fast,
fusible
FLOWER
QUILTS

Nancy Mahoney

Martingale®
& COMPANY

Fast, Fusible Flower Quilts
© 2011 by Nancy Mahoney

That Patchwork Place® is an imprint of
Martingale & Company®.

Martingale & Company
19021 120th Ave. NE, Suite 102
Bothell, WA 98011-9511
www.martingale-pub.com

Printed in China
16 15 14 13 12 11   8 7 6 5 4 3 2 1

Library of Congress Cataloging-in-Publication Data is available upon request.

ISBN: 978-1-60468-039-3

credits

President & CEO: Tom Wierzbicki

Editorial Director: Mary V. Green

Managing Editor: Tina Cook

Developmental Editor: Karen Costello Soltys

Technical Editor: Laurie Baker

Copy Editor: Melissa Bryan

Design Director: Stan Green

Production Manager: Regina Girard

Illustrator: Adrienne Smitke

Cover & Text Designer: Shelly Garrison

Photographer: Brent Kane

Special thanks to Pam and Darrel Coney, Woodinville, Washington, for generously allowing us to photograph in their beautiful yard.

mission statement

Dedicated to providing quality products and service to inspire creativity.

contents

introduction

Do you love to garden? Many quilters do—including me. I love strolling through gardens and try to visit them wherever I travel. The thrill of seeing a bold burst of color, an unexpected quiet spot to rest, or a beautiful pond or fountain stays with me long after I leave the garden. These memories are often inspirations for my own garden—and my quilts.

And, speaking of quilts, there are tons of luscious floral fabrics available today. Who can resist a chance to use them? Start with a great floral print as your inspiration, and then mix in a variety of other prints, including stripes, tone-on-tone prints, and small-scale floral coordinates and you'll be on your way to creating a quilt blooming with garden imagery.

In this book, you'll find 11 quilts with a variety of flower-themed appliqué designs. When designing quilts, I enjoy adding something unexpected—just like in my garden. Sometimes, I'll add appliquéd flower motifs to patchwork blocks, such as in "Precious Peonies" on page 14 and "Prairie Picnic" on page 42. Other times, I'll create a patchwork background, and then appliqué the flowers on top, as I did in "Amaryllis" on page 48 and "Daisy Vines" on page 66. In "Orange Marmalade" on page 54 and "Night Blooms" on page 36, I added appliqué designs to simple patchwork blocks, and then combined the appliquéd blocks with a second patchwork block to create a secondary pattern. Simple pieced sashing is used to showcase the basket blocks in "A-Tisket A-Tasket" on page 20 and "Star Flower Baskets" on page 61. In "Pink Dogwood" on page 26 and "Aunt Hattie's Garden" on page 31, the flower motifs are appliquéd to background squares; the simple designs with gentle curves make these quilts beginner friendly. And in "Pinwheel Flowers" on page 72 there's a really big surprise. Don't tell anyone, but there's no appliqué! Instead, folded flowers, buttons, and rickrack add a touch of whimsy to the tilted blocks—something a little unexpected!

I hope this book will inspire you to bring a flower garden into your home, even if you aren't blessed with a green thumb or don't have space for a garden full of flowers. Create an eye-catching array of floral quilts that will warm your heart, all year long.

quiltmaking basics

In this section, you'll find valuable information for the successful completion of your quilt. Detailed instructions for general quilting techniques are not included because there are many excellent books available at your local quilt shop or library. I encourage you to make use of those books for any additional information. All the special techniques needed to complete your quilt are covered on the following pages.

rotary cutting

The projects in this book are all designed for rotary cutting and are easily pieced by machine. Use your cutter to cut block backgrounds and borders as well as the patchwork strips and pieces in your project. All rotary-cutting measurements include ¼"-wide seam allowances. Basic rotary-cutting tools include a rotary cutter, an 18" x 24" cutting mat, a 6" x 24" acrylic ruler, and a 12½" square ruler for trimming appliqué blocks. You'll be able to make all the projects with these rulers, although I also find a 6" Bias Square® very useful for making cleanup cuts and crosscutting strips into squares.

pressing

Pressing is one of the keys to precise piecing. It's important to carefully press your work after stitching each seam. Pressing is planned so that the seam allowances will oppose one another when you sew the blocks and rows together. Occasionally, I press the seam allowances open to reduce bulk underneath appliquéd pieces. Pressing instructions are provided with each project.

Set your iron on the cotton setting and use a padded pressing surface to prevent the seam allowance from creating a ridge on the right side of the unit. Use a pressing cloth when ironing raised areas with multiple seams (which protects your fabrics from becoming glazed and shiny under the iron). To avoid possible distortion, allow the pieces to cool before moving them from the pressing surface.

squaring up blocks

After you've stitched the appliqués onto the block backgrounds, you need to square up the block, keeping the design centered. To square up an appliqué block, line up the vertical and horizontal centerlines of the block with the centerlines of the desired-size square on the square ruler. For example, the centerline of a 9" square is the 4½" line. Cut the first two sides of the square. Turn the block around and cut the other two sides.

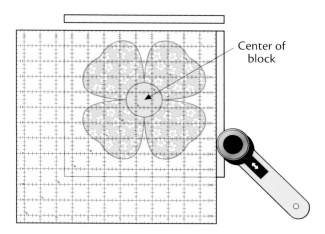

Center of block

appliqué

There are many ways to appliqué—both by hand and by machine. Each method uses different techniques. Before starting an appliqué project, you can choose which method is best for that particular project. If you're making a special heirloom quilt, you may want to use a hand-appliqué method. If, however, you're making a quilt that will receive hard wear, machine appliqué is often the best and most efficient choice. Or, you may find you'll want to use a combination of methods or techniques.

cutting background fabric

All appliqué patterns in this book are printed at full size. Because appliqué blocks tend to distort slightly and fray during stitching, for most projects you'll be cutting the block backgrounds 1" larger than the finished size and trimming them to the correct size after completing the appliqué. For instance, for a 9" finished block the background fabric would normally be cut 9½" x 9½" to allow for a ¼" seam allowance on all sides. For appliqué, the block background is cut 10" x 10" and then trimmed to 9½" x 9½". Use a rotary cutter, mat, and acrylic ruler to accurately trim the blocks.

Once you've cut your block backgrounds, mark the center of each piece by folding it in half vertically and horizontally; lightly finger-press to create centerlines.

making appliqué templates

Because you'll be making more than one of each appliqué piece, you'll find it handy to make a plastic template for each pattern segment. Templates made from clear or frosted plastic are durable and accurate, and because you can see through the plastic, you can easily trace the shapes from the patterns. Trace the pieces of each appliqué design directly from the book page to make the templates you'll need. Seam allowances are not included on templates for appliqué pieces. Prepare your templates accurately to ensure the best results. *If you're using the starch appliqué technique described on page 7, be sure to use heat-resistant template plastic when making your templates.*

To make the templates, place template plastic over each pattern piece and trace with a fine-line permanent marker, making sure to trace the lines exactly. Do not add a seam allowance. Use utility scissors to cut out the templates, cutting exactly on the drawn lines. Write the block name and pattern number on the template. This is the right side of the template. You need only one plastic template for each different pattern piece.

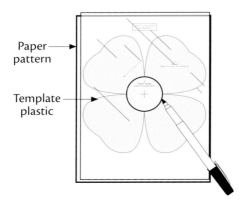

Paper pattern →

Template plastic →

a note about the patterns

Many of the appliqué patterns in this book are symmetrical and don't need to be reversed. However, a few are asymmetrical and have been drawn in reverse for starch appliqué and fusible appliqué. If you're making a placement guide of the asymmetrical patterns, you'll need to make a reverse, or mirror, image.

To make a reverse image for a placement guide, trace the entire appliqué pattern onto a piece of paper. Then place the paper on a light box or against a bright window, with the traced side toward the light. Trace the shape onto the back of the paper using a black permanent pen.

appliqué placement

An easy way to place the appliqué pieces on the block background is to make and use a placement guide underneath the background piece. To make a placement guide, follow the instructions in "A Note about the Patterns" above to trace the pattern in reverse onto a piece of paper.

I also like to draw the original cut block size around the pattern, which is helpful for centering the background square. Do this by placing a square ruler over the pattern with the midpoint of the block over the center point marked on the pattern. Trace two sides of the ruler, rotate the paper, reposition the ruler, and draw the other two sides (as described in "Squaring Up Blocks" on page 5).

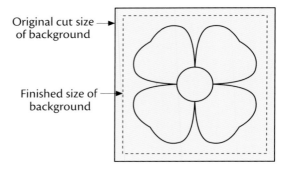

Original cut size → of background

Finished size of → background

Lay the placement guide on a table or your ironing board, and lay the background fabric over it. Carefully match the center marks and pin in place. Position the appliqués on the background, following the numerical order marked on the pattern.

When positioning the appliqué pieces on a pieced block, or if you find it difficult to see your design through the background fabric, try using a pattern overlay. A pattern overlay is helpful when the pattern has many layers of appliqué pieces, such as in "Prairie Picnic" on page 42 or "Night Blooms" on page 36.

To make a pattern overlay, use a permanent marker to trace the pattern onto a piece of clear template plastic or acetate that is the same size as your background piece. Place the plastic over the background fabric, pinning or taping it in place if desired. To position each appliqué piece, lift up the plastic and slide each piece under the appropriate marking. Remove the plastic overlay, and then pin, baste, or fuse the appliqué to the background fabric.

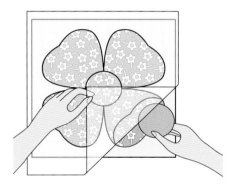

Slide appliqué shapes under the overlay to place them on the background.

starch appliqué

This appliqué technique uses a plastic template as a base to make a smooth, curved edge on an appliqué shape. This method is similar to freezer-paper appliqué, except you use a heat-resistant plastic template instead of freezer paper.

For this method you'll need a can of spray starch, a small cup, and a small (¼") foam pounce or cotton swab. Using starch saves time when preparing the pieces for appliqué, and unlike some methods that use a glue stick to temporarily hold under the seam allowances, you don't need to soak the fabrics in water to remove the starch.

With this method you can prepare all the pieces for the block and preview them before sewing. The pieces can then be stitched by hand or machine.

1. Using heat-resistant plastic, make one template of each appliqué piece, referring to "Making Appliqué Templates" on page 6.

2. Place each template right side up on the wrong side of the chosen fabric. Trace around the template using a pencil. Remove the template and cut out the shape, adding a ³⁄₁₆"-wide seam allowance all around.

no tracing

Instead of tracing around the template, place a piece of double-stick tape on the wrong side of the template. The tape will hold the template in place as you cut out the fabric shape and as you press the edges over the template. Just be careful not to iron over the piece of tape.

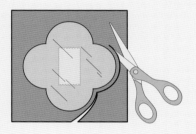

3. Place the appliqué shape flat, wrong side up, on your ironing board. Center the plastic template, right side up, on the wrong side of the appliqué fabric shape. Spray some starch into the cup. When the bubbles have all "liquified," dip the pounce or cotton swab in the starch and "paint" the starch over the seam allowance of the shape. Do not paint any edge that will lie under another piece, because that edge will not need to be basted. Wait a few minutes for the starch to penetrate the fabric. You can paint another shape, and then go back to the first shape.

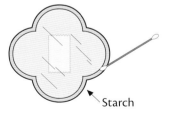

Starch

4. With the template as a guide, use a dry iron to press the seam allowance over the edge of the plastic. As you come to inside curves and inside points, clip the seam allowance to within one or two threads of the template. On outside curves, once you've achieved a smooth edge, flatten the

seam allowance into little pleats or clip the seam allowance so that the fabric overlaps.

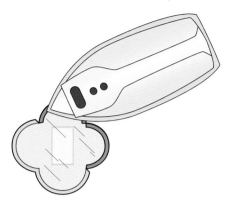

pressing tip

To keep from burning your fingers, use the pointed end of a 4"- or 6"-long bamboo skewer or a wooden orange stick to manipulate the fabric around points and curves, as well as to hold the seam allowance in place while ironing.

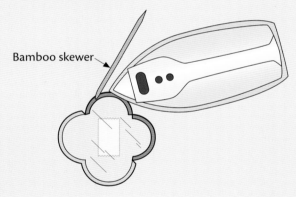

Bamboo skewer

5. For leaves and other pieces with outer points, fold one edge of the fabric leaf over the template, extending the fold beyond the point of the template. Fold the other side in the same way. If you have a little fabric "flag" sticking out, fold the flag behind the point and press with your iron. There will probably be enough starch to hold the flag in place. If not, apply a small amount and press again.

Flag

6. Allow the piece to cool, and then remove the template and press again if needed. Stitch the appliqué pieces to the block background using the invisible machine appliqué stitch described next. When the appliqué is complete, gently press and square up the block, if applicable, referring to "Squaring Up Blocks" on page 5.

invisible machine appliqué

For this method, I like to use a very small machine blanket stitch, or you can use the blind hemstitch on your machine. You'll need to adjust the length and width of the stitches to use this method effectively. When done well, it's difficult to tell the results from hand appliqué.

1. Prepare the appliqué pieces as instructed in "Starch Appliqué" on page 7.

2. Use a size 60/8 Sharp needle. Thread the top of your machine with invisible thread (size .004). Thread the bobbin with a fine (60-weight) thread that matches the background fabric or, depending on your machine, you may want to try using invisible thread in your bobbin. When threading the bobbin with regular thread, try bringing the thread through the hole in the "finger" on the bobbin (if your machine has one) to slightly increase the bobbin tension. Reduce the top tension.

3. Use an open-toe embroidery presser foot and set the machine to the blanket stitch or blind hemstitch. Shorten the stitch length so that the distance the machine sews straight (between the stitches that swing to the left) is about $1/8$". Adjust the stitch width so that the needle swings to the left no more than $1/16$".

4. Make a test piece with fabric scraps to check your stitch. Sew along the edge of a piece of folded fabric so that the straight stitches are in the background fabric, very close to the folded edge, and the swing stitch just catches the edge of the folded piece. The bobbin thread should not show on the top. Readjust the machine as necessary to achieve the proper stitch.

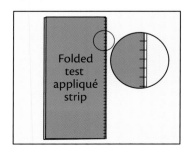

Folded test appliqué strip

5. Pin or use a little fabric glue to hold each appliqué piece in place on the block background. Position and appliqué the pieces in numerical order. Sew slowly, turning and pivoting the block as needed. Make sure the points are secured by a swing stitch on each side. Secure the thread ends by backstitching a few stitches. (The backstitches will not show on the front because of the invisible thread.)

fabric glue

There are a variety of fabric-basting glues and glue sticks available. Whichever one you choose, make sure it will wash out after the project is done.

fusible appliqué

Fusible appliqué is extra fast and easy. With this technique, there are no seam allowances to turn under. I like to use a decorative stitch, such as a machine blanket stitch or zigzag stitch, to secure the edges of the appliqué pieces. The decorative stitch adds texture, depth, and color to the project. If I don't want the stitches to show, I use a 60-weight, 100% cotton thread that matches the appliqué pieces. However, when I want the stitches to add texture to the appliquéd shape, I use a 30-weight thread in a color that either matches the appliqué pieces or provides contrast. Always make a test piece to check the size of the stitches, the thread tension, and the thread color. Make any necessary adjustments before stitching the actual appliqué pieces. I also use an open-toe embroidery foot so I can see the stitching line clearly.

Fusible web is available with smooth paper on one side and an adhesive on the reverse, or with paper on both sides and an adhesive in the middle. (There are also a few paperless fusible webs.) There are many brands on the market, but I prefer Lite Steam-A-Seam 2, which has paper on both sides. When you purchase a fusible-web product, take time to read the manufacturer's instructions. Different products call for different heat settings and handling instructions. Be careful not to allow your hot iron to directly touch fusible web that is not covered by paper or fabric. I recommend using an appliqué pressing sheet or parchment paper to protect your iron.

1. Make a plastic template for each appliqué shape as described in "Making Appliqué Templates" on page 6. Place each template on the paper side of the fusible web, right side up, and trace around it. Use a pencil or permanent marker to trace each shape the number of times indicated on the pattern, leaving about ½" between shapes.

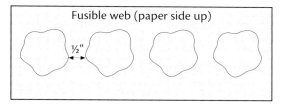
Fusible web (paper side up)
½"

2. Roughly cut out the fusible-web shape, leaving a margin of about ¼" all around the marked line. For larger pieces, or where pieces will be layered, cut out the center of the fusible-web shapes. Leave at least ¼" inside the line. This trimming allows the piece to adhere to the background while eliminating the stiffness within the shape.

3. Place the shape, fusible-web side down, on the wrong side of the appropriate appliqué fabric. Follow the manufacturer's instructions to fuse the shape to the fabric; let cool before handling.

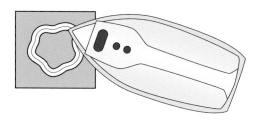

4. Cut out the fabric shape on the drawn line and remove the paper backing.

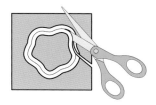

removing the paper

If you haven't cut away the center of the fusible web, try this tip. After cutting out the fabric shape along the drawn line, use a pin to score the paper in the center of the shape. Fold the shape along the scored line to loosen the paper, and then remove it from the fabric.

5. Using your pattern as a guide, position the appliqué shapes, adhesive side down, on the right side of the background fabric in numerical order and press.

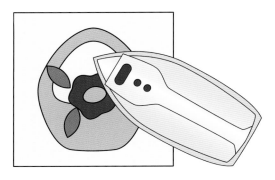

6. When all the pieces have been fused in place, finish the edges with a decorative stitch, such as a machine blanket stitch. Sew so that the straight stitches are in the background fabric, very close to the appliqué edge, and the swing stitch is in the appliqué piece. You can also use a narrow zigzag stitch on the edges of the appliqués.

Blanket stitch   Zigzag stitch

hand appliqué

I greatly admire the beauty of hand appliqué and appreciate the flexibility it gives you to enjoy a take-along project. The starch appliqué technique described on page 7 works well with hand appliqué. When I want a take-along project, I prepare the appliqué pieces using the starch appliqué method, and then hand appliqué them in place. I especially like this method for circles in the center of appliquéd designs or pieced blocks, such as the appliquéd blocks in "Orange Marmalade" on page 54. For information on hand appliqué techniques, check out appliqué books available at your local quilt shop.

adding borders

Borders can be simple strips of one or more fabrics. They can also be pieced or appliquéd and used in combination with plain strips. I've used a variety of border styles for the quilts in this book. Of course, you may choose to omit a border, but that will require yardage adjustments which have not been provided.

Prepare border strips a few inches longer than you will actually need, and then trim them to the correct length once you know the dimensions of the center of your quilt top. To find the correct measurement for the border strips, always measure through the center of the quilt, not at the outside edges. This ensures that the borders are of equal length on opposite sides of the quilt and helps keep your quilt square.

For borders wider than 3", I usually cut the strips on the lengthwise grain (parallel to the selvage) so that they don't stretch and don't have to be pieced. This is especially true when I'm using a large-scale print for the outer border, because it can be harder to disguise the seams. I also prefer to attach the side border strips first, and then add strips to the two remaining edges.

If you choose, you can cut strips on the crosswise grain, selvage to selvage, and join them end to end with a diagonal seam to achieve the desired length. Press the seam allowances open so that they lie flat and are less conspicuous. Try to place the seams randomly around the quilt to make them less noticeable.

For borders less than 3" wide, I cut the strips from the crosswise grain and join them end to end as described before.

Follow these instructions when adding borders with butted corners to your quilt.

1. Lay two strips across the center of the quilt top from top to bottom. Trim both ends even with the raw edge of the quilt.

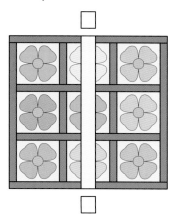

2. Mark the center of the border strips and the center of the sides of the quilt top. Pin the borders to the sides of the quilt top, matching centers and ends. Ease or slightly stretch the quilt top to fit the border strip as necessary. Sew the side borders in place with a $\frac{1}{4}$"-wide seam allowance and press the seam allowances toward the border strips.

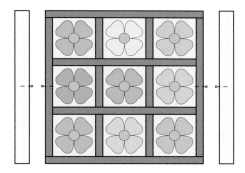

Mark centers.

3. Repeat the process for the top and bottom borders, measuring across the borders you just added.

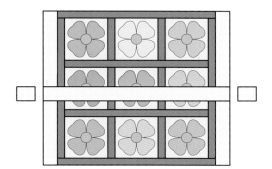

finishing techniques

Once your quilt top is done, you're ready to move on to the finishing stages.

backing and batting

For the quilt backing, cut a piece of fabric 4" to 6" larger than the quilt top (2" to 3" on all sides). For quilts wider than the width of your fabric, you'll need to piece the backing. For most quilts in this book, I've listed enough backing fabric to piece the backing with one seam, leaving sufficient leftover fabric to cut a hanging sleeve, if desired. When piecing the backing, be sure to trim off the selvages before sewing the pieces together. Press the seam allowances open to reduce bulk.

Many types of batting are available today. The type you select will depend on whether you plan to hand or machine quilt your quilt top. For machine quilting, a cotton batting works best, because it won't move or slip between the quilt top and the backing. Whatever type of batting you choose, the piece should be large enough to allow an extra 2" around all edges of the quilt top.

If you plan to have your quilt professionally machine quilted, check with the long-arm quilter to see which type of batting is preferred and how you should prepare your backing.

layering and basting

All the quilts in this book are machine quilted. If you plan to machine quilt your quilt using your home sewing machine, follow these instructions to sandwich your layers together.

Before you layer the quilt, give the quilt top and backing a careful pressing. Remove the batting from its package and let it relax for at least 24 hours, or place it in your dryer on a cool setting to eliminate wrinkles.

Next, spread the backing, wrong side up, on a flat, clean surface. Anchor the backing with pins or masking tape, taking care not to stretch the fabric out of shape. Center the batting over the backing, smoothing out any wrinkles. Center the pressed quilt top, right side up, over the batting, smoothing out any wrinkles and making sure the edges of the quilt top are parallel to the edges of the backing. Note that you should always smooth outward from the center and along straight lines to ensure that the blocks and borders remain straight.

For machine quilting, baste the layers with size #2 rustproof safety pins. Place pins 3" to 4" apart, trying to avoid areas where you intend to quilt. Finish by machine basting around the edges about ⅛" from the edge of the quilt top.

spray basting

Instead of pin basting, try using a temporary spray adhesive. Be sure to follow the manufacturer's instructions for whichever product you use. I like Sulky KK 2000 because it's odorless, clear, and nontoxic. It also has a tighter spray pattern, which reduces overspray. I prepare the backing the same as I would for pin basting. I spray the backing before spreading out the batting. Then I spray the batting, spread out the quilt top over it, and gently pat all over the top, making sure the edges of the quilt top are parallel to the edges of the backing.

quilting

As a general rule, no unquilted areas should exceed 4" x 4". In addition, check the package of the batting that you're using for recommendations concerning the appropriate amount of quilting. The density of quilting should be similar throughout the entire quilt so that the quilt will remain square and not become distorted. For more information on machine quilting, refer to *Machine Quilting Made Easy!* by Maurine Noble (Martingale & Company, 1994).

squaring up your quilt

When you complete the quilting, you'll need to trim the excess backing and batting as well as square up your quilt before sewing on the binding. Make sure all the basting threads or pins have been removed, but leave the basting stitches around the outer edges. Align a ruler with the seam line of the outer border and measure the width of the outer border in several places. Using the narrowest measurement, position a ruler along the seam line of the outer border, and trim the excess batting and backing from all four sides. Use a large, square ruler to square up each corner.

binding

The binding offers a wonderful opportunity to add to the overall look of your quilt. If you want the binding to "disappear," use the same fabric for the binding as for the outer border. If you prefer a "framed" effect, select a binding fabric that is different from the outer border.

Strips for binding are generally cut 2" to 2½" wide, depending on your preference for binding width and your choice of batting. (I used 2"-wide strips for the quilts in this book.) Cut enough strips to go around the perimeter of your quilt plus about 10" extra for making seams and turning corners.

1. To make one long, continuous strip, place the strips at right angles to each other, right sides together, and stitch across the corner as shown. Trim the excess fabric, leaving a ¼"-wide seam allowance, and press the seam allowances open.

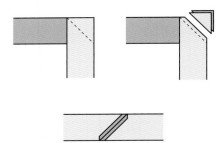

2. Press the long strip in half lengthwise, wrong sides together and raw edges aligned.

3. Starting on the bottom edge of the quilt (not at a corner), align the raw edge of the strip with the raw edge of the quilt. Beginning 8" from the end of the strip, use a walking foot and a ¼"-wide seam allowance to stitch the binding strip to the quilt. Stop ¼" from the first corner and backstitch. Remove the quilt from the machine.

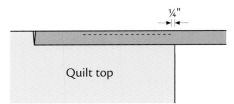

Quilt top

4. Turn the quilt; fold the binding straight up and away from the quilt so that the fold forms a 45° angle. Fold the binding back down onto itself, even with the edge of the quilt top, and pin as shown to create an angled pleat at the corner. Begin with a backstitch at the fold of the binding and continue stitching along the edge of the quilt top, mitering each corner as you come to it.

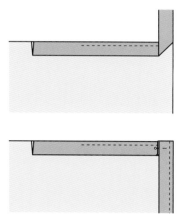

5. Stop stitching about 10" from the point where you started and backstitch. Remove the quilt from the machine. Place the quilt on a flat surface and overlap the ending tail on top of the beginning tail. Mark the binding strips so that the overlap is 2" (or the width of your cut binding). Trim each end of the binding at the marked points.

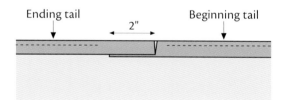

6. Unfold both ends of the binding strip, and then align them at right angles, right sides together as shown. Pin the ends together, and then sew diagonally from corner to corner. Trim the excess fabric, leaving a ¼" seam allowance, and press the seam allowances open. Refold the binding strip; press and sew it in place on the quilt.

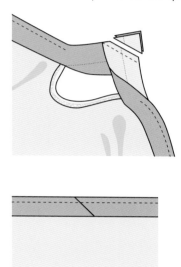

7. Turn the binding to the back of the quilt. Using thread to match the binding, hand stitch the binding in place so that the folded edge covers the row of machine stitching. At each corner, fold the binding to form a miter on the back of the quilt.

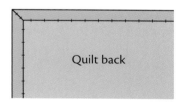

precious peonies

Pretty floral fabrics, graceful appliqué, and simple pieced blocks combine to make this sweet quilt the perfect choice for any decor. Use it as a wall hanging to brighten a room, or snuggle under it and dream of summer on a cold winter day.

Finished Quilt Size: 68½" x 68½"

Finished Block Size: 16½" x 16½"

materials

Yardages are based on 42"-wide fabrics.

2¼ yards of dark green floral for outer border and binding

1⅔ yards of cream print for blocks and middle border

1⅛ yards of pink floral for blocks and sashing squares

⅞ yard of light green floral for sashing and inner border

½ yard of pink tone-on-tone print for blocks

½ yard of green fabric 1 for blocks

½ yard of green fabric 2 for leaf appliqués

½ yard of medium pink fabric for flower appliqués

¼ yard of dark pink fabric for flower appliqués

4½ yards of fabric for backing

75" x 75" piece of batting

2 yards of 16"-wide lightweight fusible web (optional)

cutting

Cut all strips across the width of the fabric unless indicated otherwise.

From the pink floral, cut:
3 strips, 8¼" x 42"; crosscut into:
    9 squares, 8¼" x 8¼"
    4 squares, 2" x 2"
3 strips, 3¼" x 42"; crosscut into 36 squares, 3¼" x 3¼"

From the cream print, cut:
3 strips, 6⅜" x 42"; crosscut into 18 squares, 6⅜" x 6⅜". Cut each square in half diagonally to yield 36 half-square triangles.
7 strips, 3⅝" x 42"; crosscut into 72 squares, 3⅝" x 3⅝". Cut each square in half diagonally to yield 144 half-square triangles.
6 strips, 1½" x 42"

From the pink tone-on-tone print, cut:
4 strips, 3⅝" x 42"; crosscut into 36 squares, 3⅝" x 3⅝". Cut each square in half diagonally to yield 72 half-square triangles.

From green fabric 1, cut:
2 strips, 6¾" x 42"; crosscut into 9 squares, 6¾" x 6¾". Cut each square into quarters diagonally to yield 36 triangles.

From the light green floral, cut:
12 strips, 2" x 42"; crosscut 6 of *the strips* into 12 strips, 2" x 17"

From the *lengthwise grain* of the dark green floral, cut:
2 strips, 5¾" x 72"
2 strips, 5¾" x 61"
5 strips, 2" x 58"

Pieced and appliquéd by Nancy Mahoney; machine quilted by Nan Moore

making the blocks

1. Fold each pink floral 8¼" square in half vertically and horizontally and finger-press the folds to establish centering lines. Fold each cream 6⅜" triangle in half and finger-press the fold to mark the center on the long side. Sew cream triangles to opposite sides of a pink floral square, aligning the creased lines. Press the seam allowances toward the triangles. Sew cream triangles to the remaining sides of the square to complete a center unit. Press the seam allowances toward the triangles. The unit should measure 11½" square. Make nine center units.

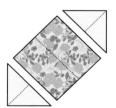
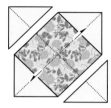

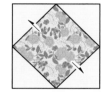

Make 9.

2. Join a cream 3⅝" triangle to a pink tone-on-tone triangle to make a triangle-square unit. Press the seam allowances toward the pink triangle. The unit should measure 3¼" square. Make 72 units.

Make 72.

3. Sew cream 3⅝" triangles to the short sides of a green fabric 1 triangle to make a flying-geese unit. Press the seam allowances toward the cream triangles. The unit should measure 3¼" x 6". Make 36 units.

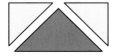

Make 36.

4. Join two triangle squares and one flying-geese unit as shown to make a side unit. Press the seam allowances toward the pink triangles. Make 36 units.

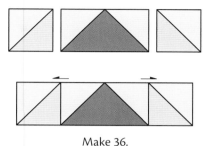

Make 36.

5. Lay out four pink floral 3¼" squares, four side units from step 4, and one center unit from step 1 as shown. Sew the pieces together into rows, and then sew the rows together to complete the block. Press the seam allowances as indicated. Make nine blocks.

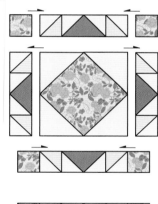

Make 9.

adding the appliqué

Use your preferred method or refer to "Appliqué" on page 5 for more information on starch appliqué and fusible-web machine appliqué. Refer to the diagram on page 18 for appliqué placement.

1. Using the patterns on page 19 and your preferred method, make 36 green fabric 2 leaves, 36 medium pink outer petals, and 36 dark pink center petals.

2. Appliqué the shapes in place on each block, working in numerical order.

Appliqué placement

assembling the quilt top

1. Sew three blocks and two light green floral 2" x 17" sashing strips together, alternating them as shown. Press the seam allowances toward the sashing strips. Make three block rows.

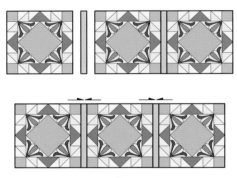

Make 3.

2. Sew three light green floral 2" x 17" sashing strips and two pink floral 2" squares together, alternating them as shown. Press the seam allowances toward the sashing strips. Make two sashing rows.

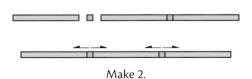

Make 2.

3. Refer to the quilt assembly diagram to join the block rows and sashing rows. Press the seam allowances toward the sashing rows.

4. Join the remaining light green 2"-wide strips end to end to make a long strip. Refer to "Adding Borders" on page 10 to measure, cut, and sew the strips for the inner border, attaching them to the sides, and then to the top and bottom edges of the quilt top.

5. Join the cream 1½"-wide strips end to end to make a long strip. Measure, cut, and sew the strips for the middle border, attaching them to the sides, and then to the top and bottom edges of the quilt top.

6. Using the dark green floral 5¾"-wide strips, measure and cut the shorter strips and sew them to the sides of the quilt top. Repeat to add the longer strips to the top and bottom edges of the quilt top to complete the outer border.

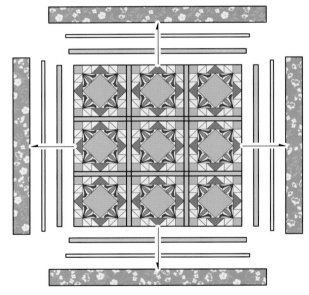

Quilt assembly

finishing

Refer to "Finishing Techniques" on page 11. Cut and piece the backing fabric, and then layer the quilt top with batting and backing. After basting the layers together, hand or machine quilt as desired; see the quilting suggestion at right. Trim the batting and backing so that the edges are even with the quilt top. Using the dark green floral 2"-wide strips, make and attach the binding.

Quilting diagram

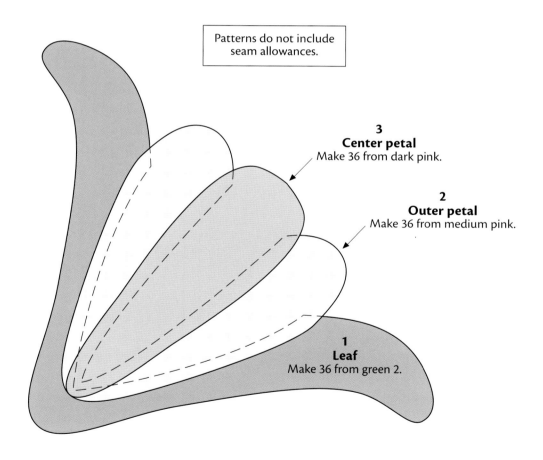

Patterns do not include seam allowances.

3
Center petal
Make 36 from dark pink.

2
Outer petal
Make 36 from medium pink.

1
Leaf
Make 36 from green 2.

a-tisket a-tasket

A-tisket a-tasket, you won't need a green thumb to fill your baskets with pretty posies. The easy appliqué baskets and quick nine-patch units in this fun quilt make it an ideal choice for beginning or experienced quilters alike.

Finished Quilt Size: 47" x 59"
Finished Block Size: 9" x 9"

materials

Yardages are based on 42"-wide fabrics.

1⅞ yards of cream print for block backgrounds, sashing, and nine-patch units

1⅔ yards of black-and-red floral for border*

⅞ yard of red tone-on-tone print for sashing, nine-patch units, and flower appliqués

⅞ yard of gold tone-on-tone print for basket appliqués and flower-center appliqués

⅝ yard of green striped fabric for leaf appliqués and binding

3¼ yards of fabric for backing

53" x 65" piece of batting

2 yards of 16"-wide lightweight fusible web (optional)

*Yardage amount is for one-piece lengthwise-cut border strips. If you don't mind seams in your border, ⅞ yard is sufficient to cut crosswise strips.

cutting

Cut all strips across the width of the fabric unless indicated otherwise.

From the cream print, cut:
3 strips, 10" x 42"; crosscut into 12 squares, 10" x 10"
20 strips, 1½" x 42"

From the red tone-on-tone print, cut:
13 strips, 1½" x 42"

From the *lengthwise grain* of the black-and-red floral, cut:
4 strips, 4¼" x 54" (or 6 strips, 4¼" x 42", from the crosswise grain)

From the green striped fabric, cut:
6 strips, 2" x 42"

making the basket blocks

Use your preferred method or refer to "Appliqué" on page 5 for more information on starch appliqué and fusible-web machine appliqué. Refer to the diagram for appliqué placement.

1. Using the patterns on page 25 and your preferred method, make 12 gold baskets, 36 green striped leaves, 12 red flowers, and 12 gold flower centers.

2. Fold each cream 10" square in half vertically and horizontally to establish centering lines. Working in numerical order, appliqué the shapes in place on each square. Make 12 blocks.

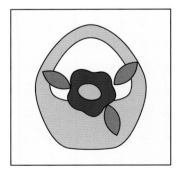

Appliqué placement

3. Trim each block to measure 9½" square, referring to "Squaring Up Blocks" on page 5.

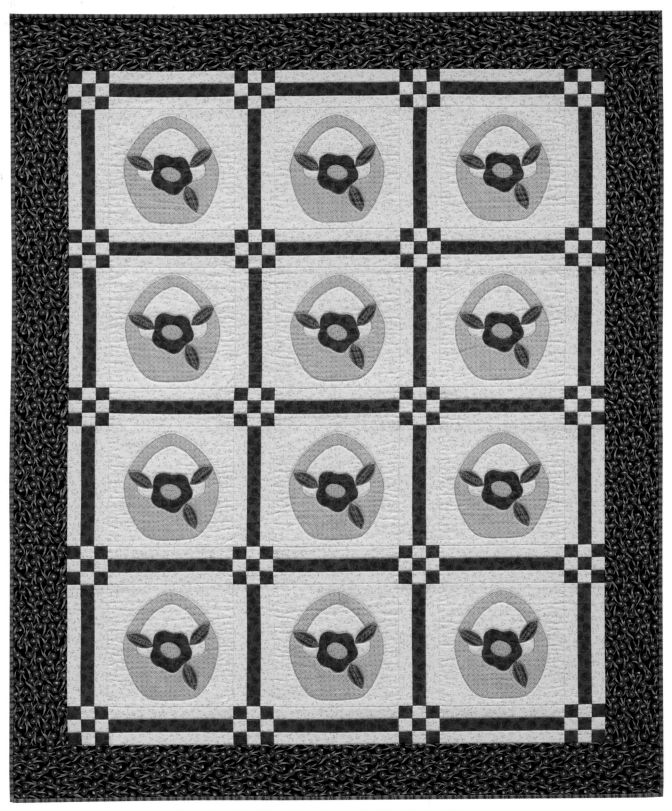

Pieced, appliquéd, and machine quilted by Nancy Mahoney

making the sashing strips and nine-patch units

1. Join two cream strips and one red strip along their long edges to make a strip set. Press the seam allowances toward the red strip. Make nine strip sets. Crosscut eight strip sets into 31 sashing strips, 9½" long. Crosscut the remaining strip set into 20 segments, 1½" wide.

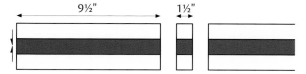

Make 9 strip sets.
Cut 31 sashing strips, 9½" wide,
and 20 segments, 1½" wide.

2. Join two red strips and one cream strip along their long edges to make a strip set. Press the seam allowances toward the red strips. Make two strip sets. Crosscut them into 40 segments, 1½" wide.

Make 2 strip sets.
Cut 40 segments, 1½" wide.

3. Lay out two segments from step 2 and one 1½" segment from step 1 as shown. Join the segments to make a nine-patch unit. Press the seam allowances away from the center segment. Make 20 units.

Make 20.

assembling the quilt top

1. Sew three blocks and four 9½" sashing strips together, alternating them as shown. Press the seam allowances toward the sashing strips. Make four block rows.

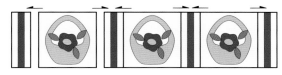

Make 4.

2. Sew three 9½" sashing strips and four nine-patch units together, alternating them as shown. Press the seam allowances toward the sashing strips. Make five sashing rows.

Make 5.

3. Refer to the quilt assembly diagram to alternately join the block rows and sashing rows. Press the seam allowances toward the sashing rows.

4. Refer to "Adding Borders" on page 10 to measure, cut, and sew the black-and-red floral 4¼"-wide strips for the border, joining them to the sides, and then to the top and bottom edges of the quilt top.

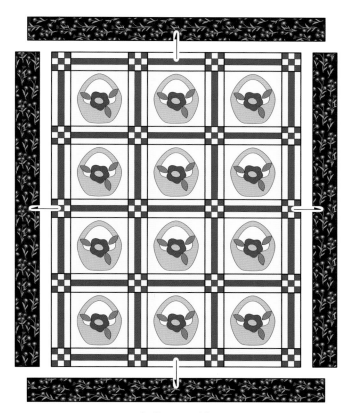

Quilt assembly

finishing

Refer to "Finishing Techniques" on page 11. Cut and piece the backing fabric, and then layer the quilt top with batting and backing. After basting the layers together, hand or machine quilt as desired; see the quilting suggestion at right. Trim the batting and backing so that the edges are even with the quilt top. Using the green striped 2"-wide strips, make and attach the binding.

Quilting diagram

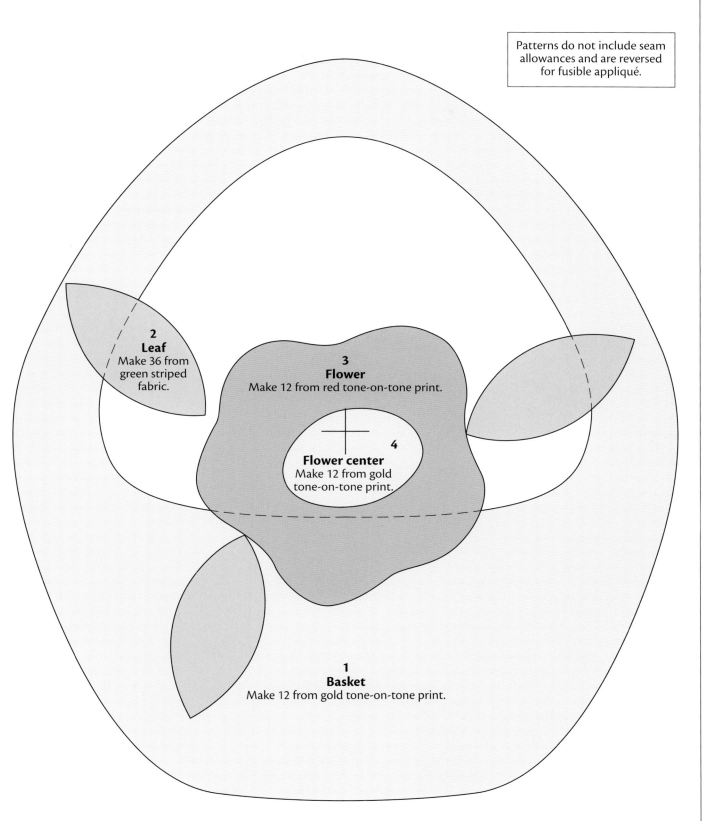

Patterns do not include seam allowances and are reversed for fusible appliqué.

2
Leaf
Make 36 from green striped fabric.

3
Flower
Make 12 from red tone-on-tone print.

4
Flower center
Make 12 from gold tone-on-tone print.

1
Basket
Make 12 from gold tone-on-tone print.

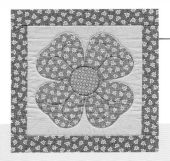

pink dogwood

The dogwood is one of my favorite springtime flowers. It symbolizes durability and undiminished love. Display this wall hanging to enjoy springtime all year long, or make it for a cherished grandchild as a symbol of your love.

Finished Quilt Size: 43½" x 43½"
Finished Block Size: 9" x 9"

materials

Yardages are based on 42"-wide fabrics.
Fat eighths measure 9" x 21".

1⅛ yards of green floral for sashing, first and fourth borders, and binding

1 yard of cream solid for block backgrounds

½ yard of light pink plaid for second border

⅓ yard of dark pink print for third border

1 fat eighth of gold checked fabric for flower center appliqués

9" x 9" square *each* of 9 assorted pink prints for flower appliqués

3 yards of fabric for backing

50" x 50" piece of batting

2¼ yards of 16"-wide lightweight fusible web (optional)

cutting

Cut all strips across the width of the fabric.

From the cream solid, cut:
3 strips, 10" x 42"; crosscut into 9 squares, 10" x 10"

From the green floral, cut:
8 strips, 2" x 42"; crosscut into:
    2 strips, 2" x 33½"
    4 strips, 2" x 30½"
    6 strips, 2" x 9½"
5 strips, 2" x 42"
5 strips, 1½" x 42"

From the light pink plaid, cut:
4 strips, 3½" x 42"

From the dark pink print, cut:
5 strips, 1½" x 42"

appliquéing the blocks

Use your preferred method or refer to "Appliqué" on page 5 for more information on starch appliqué and fusible-web machine appliqué. Refer to the diagram for appliqué placement.

1. Using the patterns on page 30 and your preferred method, make nine pink flowers and nine gold flower centers.

2. Fold each cream 10" square in half vertically and horizontally to establish centering lines. Center a pink flower, and then a gold flower center on each cream square and appliqué them in place. Make nine blocks.

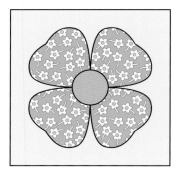

Appliqué placement

3. Trim each block to measure 9½" square, referring to "Squaring Up Blocks" on page 5.

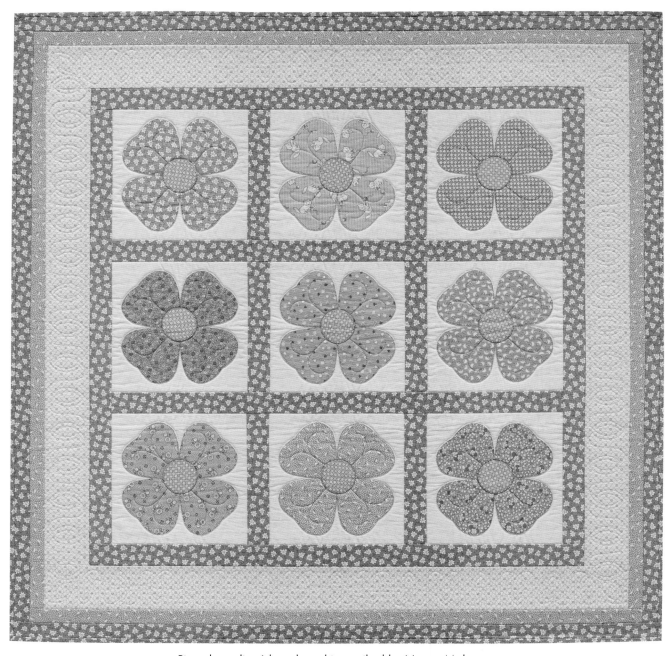

Pieced, appliquéd, and machine quilted by Nancy Mahoney

assembling the quilt top

1. Sew three blocks and two green floral 2" x 9½" sashing strips together, alternating them as shown. Press the seam allowances toward the sashing strips. Make three block rows.

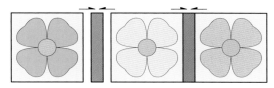

Make 3.

2. Sew the block rows and two of the green floral 2" x 30½" sashing strips together, alternating them as shown. Press the seam allowances toward the sashing strips. Sew the remaining green floral 30½"-long strips to opposite sides of the quilt center for the first border. Then sew the green floral 33½"-long strips to the top and bottom edges of the quilt top. Press the seam allowances toward the border strips.

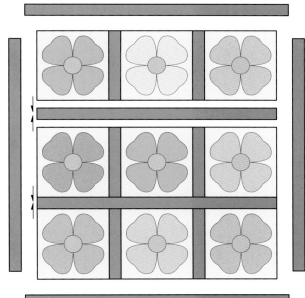

3. Refer to "Adding Borders" on page 10 and the quilt assembly diagram to measure, cut, and sew the light pink plaid 3½"-wide strips, joining them to the sides, and then to the top and bottom edges of the quilt top for the second border. Press the seam allowances toward the just-added border strips.

4. Sew the dark pink 1½"-wide strips together end to end to make a long strip. Refer to "Adding Borders" to measure, cut, and sew the strips for the third border. Press the seam allowances toward the just-added border strips.

5. Sew the green floral 1½"-wide strips together end to end to make a long strip. Measure, cut, and sew the strips for the fourth border. Press the seam allowances toward the just-added border strips.

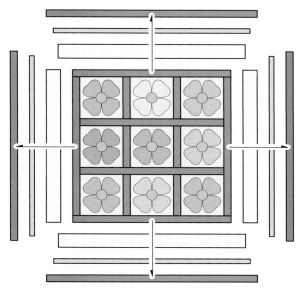

Quilt assembly

finishing

Refer to "Finishing Techniques" on page 11. Cut and piece the backing fabric, and then layer the quilt top with batting and backing. After basting the layers together, hand or machine quilt as desired; see the quilting suggestion below. Trim the batting and backing so that the edges are even with the quilt top. Using the green floral 2"-wide strips, make and attach the binding.

Quilting diagram

Patterns do not include
seam allowances.

1
Flower
Make 9 from assorted pink prints.

2
Flower center
Make 9 from gold checked fabric.

aunt hattie's garden

Easy appliqué and 1930s-style prints hearken back to sweet family memories. Gather your stash of reproduction prints and get ready to cultivate your own garden of blooms.

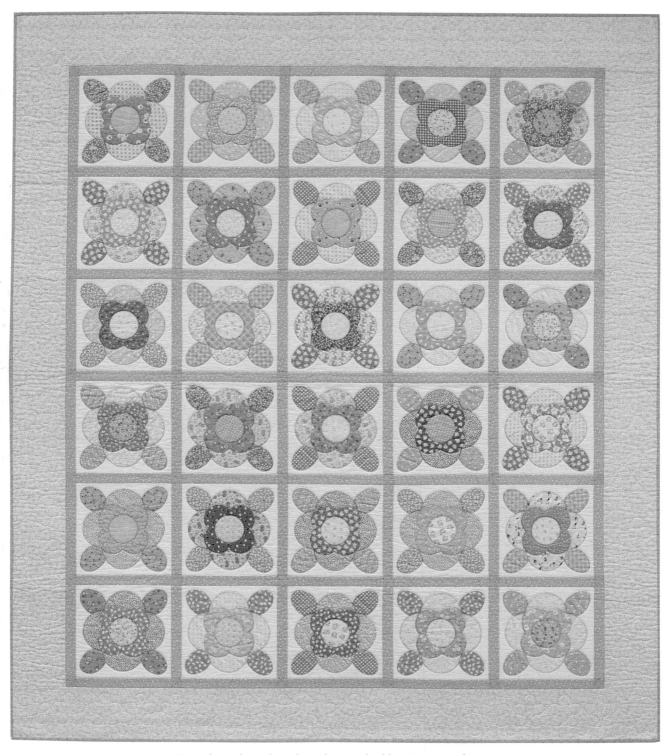

Pieced, appliquéd, and machine quilted by Nancy Mahoney

Finished Quilt Size: 61½" x 71½"

Finished Block Size: 9" x 9"

materials

Yardages are based on 42"-wide fabrics. Fat quarters measure 18" x 21".

2½ yards of cream solid for block background

2 yards of light aqua print for border*

8" x 8" square *each* of 10 assorted light blue prints, 10 assorted lavender prints, and 10 assorted light pink prints for flower appliqués

7" x 7" square *each* of 10 assorted dark blue prints, 10 assorted purple prints, and 10 assorted dark pink prints for flower appliqués

5 fat quarters of assorted green prints for leaf appliqués

⅞ yard of dark aqua print for sashing

⅝ yard of red print for sashing squares and binding

3" x 11" rectangle *each* of 8 to 10 assorted yellow prints for flower center appliqués

4¼ yards of fabric for backing

68" x 78" piece of batting

7¼ yards of 16"-wide lightweight fusible web (optional)

*Yardage amount is for one-piece lengthwise-cut border strips. If you don't mind seams in your outer border, 1¼ yards is sufficient to cut crosswise strips.

cutting

Cut all strips across the width of the fabric unless indicated otherwise.

From the cream solid, cut:
8 strips, 10" x 42"; crosscut into 30 squares, 10" x 10"

From the dark aqua print, cut:
18 strips, 1½" x 42"; crosscut into 71 strips, 1½" x 9½"

From the red print, cut:
7 strips, 2" x 42"

2 strips, 1½" x 42"; crosscut into 42 squares, 1½" x 1½"

From the *lengthwise grain* of the light aqua print, cut:
4 strips, 5½" x 65" (or 7 strips, 5½" x 42", from the crosswise grain)

appliquéing the blocks

Use your preferred method or refer to "Appliqué" on page 5 for more information on starch appliqué and fusible-web machine appliqué. Refer to the diagram for appliqué placement.

1. Using the patterns on page 35 and your preferred method, make 30 light blue, lavender, and light pink outer flowers; 30 dark blue, purple, and dark pink inner flowers; 30 sets of four matching green leaves; and 30 yellow flower centers.

2. Fold each cream 10" square in half vertically and horizontally to establish centering lines. Working in numerical order, position the shapes on each square and appliqué them in place. Make 30 blocks.

Appliqué placement

3. Trim each block to measure 9½" square, referring to "Squaring Up Blocks" on page 5.

assembling the quilt top

1. Sew five blocks and six dark aqua sashing strips together, alternating them as shown. Press the seam allowances toward the sashing strips. Make six block rows.

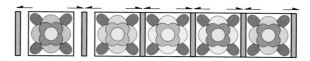

Make 6.

2. Sew five dark aqua sashing strips and six red squares together, alternating them as shown. Press the seam allowances toward the sashing strips. Make seven sashing rows.

Make 7.

3. Refer to the quilt assembly diagram to join the block rows and sashing rows; press the seam allowances toward the sashing rows.

4. Refer to "Adding Borders" on page 10 to measure, cut, and sew the light aqua 5½"-wide border strips, attaching them to the sides, and then to the top and bottom edges of the quilt top.

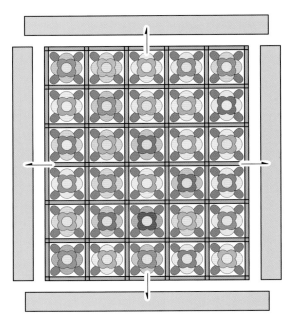

Quilt assembly

finishing

Refer to "Finishing Techniques" on page 11. Cut and piece the backing fabric, and then layer the quilt top with batting and backing. After basting the layers together, hand or machine quilt as desired; see the quilting suggestion below. Trim the batting and backing so that the edges are even with the quilt top. Using the red 2"-wide strips, make and attach the binding.

Quilting diagram

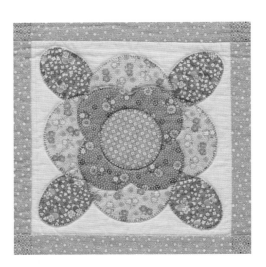

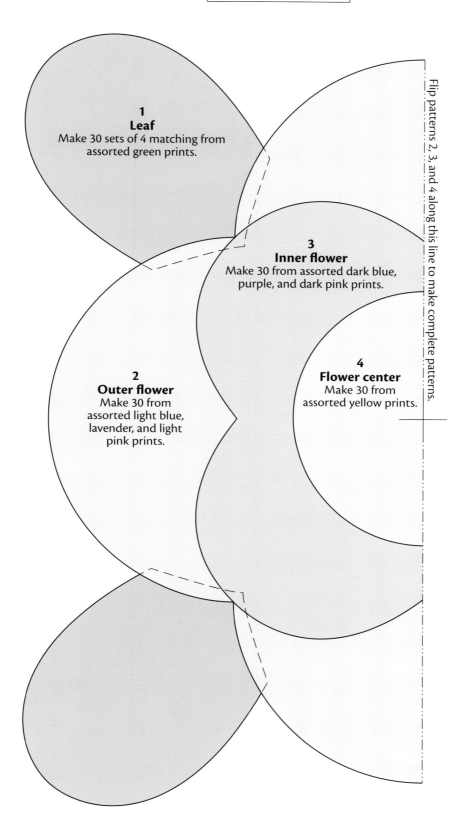

Patterns do not include seam allowances.

1
Leaf
Make 30 sets of 4 matching from assorted green prints.

3
Inner flower
Make 30 from assorted dark blue, purple, and dark pink prints.

2
Outer flower
Make 30 from assorted light blue, lavender, and light pink prints.

4
Flower center
Make 30 from assorted yellow prints.

Flip patterns 2, 3, and 4 along this line to make complete patterns.

night blooms

Hothouse blossoms stand out against a background of cool blues in this striking quilt. Nine Patch blocks, Snowball blocks, and simple appliqué come together in a quick and easy project for all skill levels. A scrap bag of batiks is all you need to whip up this winning quilt.

Finished Quilt Size: 62½" x 80½"
Finished Block Size: 9" x 9"

materials

Yardages are based on 42"-wide fabrics. Fat quarters measure 18" x 21" and fat eighths measure 9" x 21".

1 fat quarter *each* of 9 assorted medium to dark blue batiks for blocks

2¼ yards of light blue batik for blocks

2⅛ yards of medium blue batik for blocks, inner border, and outer border

1 fat eighth *each* of 8 assorted red or orange batiks for flower appliqués

1 fat eighth *each* of 6 assorted bright green batiks for leaf appliqués

⅓ yard of lime green batik for middle border

6" x 12" rectangle *each* of 3 assorted yellow batiks for flower center appliqués

3" x 12" rectangle of brown batik for flower center appliqués

⅝ yard of dark blue batik for binding

5¼ yards of fabric for backing

69" x 86" piece of batting

2¼ yards of 16"-wide lightweight fusible web (optional)

cutting

Cut all strips across the width of the fabric unless indicated otherwise.

From *each* of the 9 assorted medium to dark blue batik fat quarters, cut:
16 squares, 3½" x 3½" (144 total)

From the light blue batik, cut:
5 strips, 9½" x 42"; crosscut into 17 squares, 9½" x 9½"
7 strips, 3½" x 3½"; crosscut into 72 squares, 3½" x 3½"

From the *lengthwise grain* of the medium blue batik for blocks and borders, cut:
2 strips, 6¾" x 70"
2 strips, 6¾" x 66"
2 strips, 2" x 66"
2 strips, 2" x 51"
14 squares, 3½" x 3½"

From the lime green batik, cut:
6 strips, 1¼" x 42"

From the dark blue batik for binding, cut:
8 strips, 2" x 42"

making the nine patch blocks

Using the 3½" squares from the assorted medium to dark blue fat quarters, the medium blue batik for blocks and borders, and the light blue batik, lay out five medium or dark blue squares and four light blue squares in a nine-patch arrangement. Sew the squares together into rows. Press the seam allowances toward the darker squares. Sew the rows together and press the seam allowances outward. Make 18 blocks.

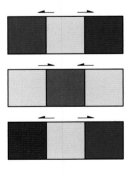

Make 18.

making the snowball blocks

1. Draw a diagonal line from corner to corner on the wrong side of the remaining medium to dark blue 3½" squares. Place marked squares in diagonally opposite corners

Pieced, appliquéd, and machine quilted by Nancy Mahoney

of a light blue 9½" square. Sew along the lines and trim the corner fabric, leaving a ¼" seam allowance. Press the seam allowances toward the resulting triangles.

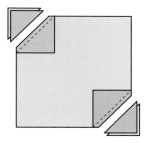 

2. Place marked squares on the two remaining corners and sew along the lines. Trim and press the seam allowances toward the resulting triangles.

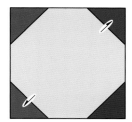

3. Repeat steps 1 and 2 to make 17 blocks.

adding the appliqué

Use your preferred method or refer to "Appliqué" on page 5 for more information on starch appliqué and fusible-web machine appliqué. Refer to the diagram for appliqué placement.

1. Using the patterns on page 41 and your preferred method, make 17 sets of four matching bright green leaves, 17 red or orange flowers, 17 yellow large flower centers, and 17 brown small flower centers.

2. Fold each Snowball block in half vertically and horizontally to establish centering lines. Working in numerical order, appliqué the shapes in place on each block.

Appliqué placement

assembling the quilt top

1. Lay out the Nine Patch blocks and appliquéd Snowball blocks in seven rows of five blocks each, alternating the blocks as shown. When you're pleased with the arrangement, sew the blocks together into rows. Press the seam allowances toward the Nine Patch blocks. Sew the rows together and press the seam allowances in one direction.

2. Refer to "Adding Borders" on page 10 and the quilt assembly diagram on page 40 to measure, cut, and sew the medium blue 2"-wide strips for the inner border, using the longer strips for the sides and the shorter strips for the top and bottom edges of the quilt top. Press the seam allowances toward the border strips.

3. Sew the lime green 1¼"-wide strips together end to end to make a long strip. Refer to "Adding Borders" to measure, cut, and sew the strips for the middle border. Press the seam allowances toward the just-added border strips.

4. Repeat step 2 with the medium blue 6¾"-wide strips to add the outer border. Press the seam allowances toward the just-added border strips.

Quilt assembly

finishing

Refer to "Finishing Techniques" on page 11. Cut and piece the backing fabric, and then layer the quilt top with batting and backing. After basting the layers together, hand or machine quilt as desired; see the quilting suggestion below. Trim the batting and backing so that the edges are even with the quilt top. Using the dark blue 2"-wide strips, make and attach the binding.

Quilting diagram

grandma's blooms

You'll need to make only nine blocks to wrap your little bundle of joy in this charming baby quilt. Pieced, appliquéd, and machine quilted by Nancy Mahoney.

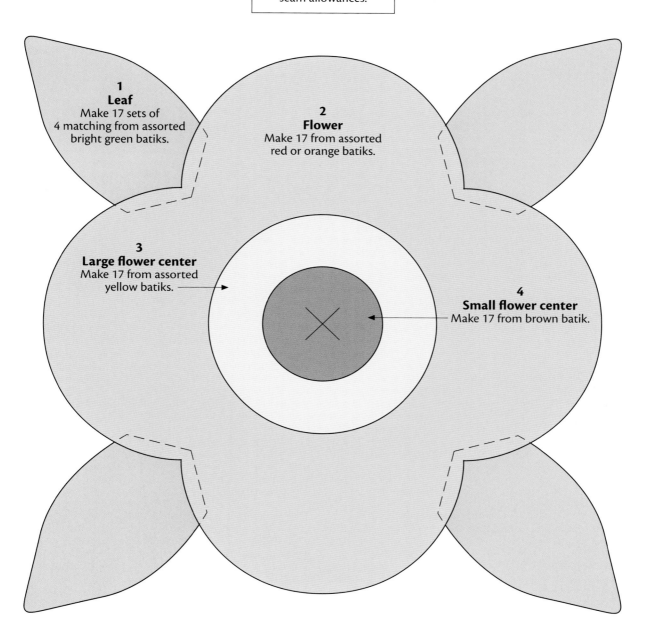

Patterns do not include seam allowances.

1
Leaf
Make 17 sets of 4 matching from assorted bright green batiks.

2
Flower
Make 17 from assorted red or orange batiks.

3
Large flower center
Make 17 from assorted yellow batiks.

4
Small flower center
Make 17 from brown batik.

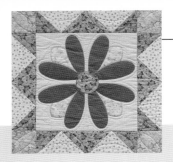

prairie picnic

This cheerful quilt is sure to bring an extra ray of sunshine to your summer gatherings. Prairie flowers appliquéd in the center of patchwork blocks and fun prairie points make this quilt a favorite addition at any picnic.

Finished Quilt Size: 53⅝" x 71"

Finished Block Size: 16½" x 16½"

materials

Yardages are based on 42"-wide fabrics.

2 yards of dark red checked fabric for flower appliqués, prairie points, and binding

2 yards of multicolored floral for outer border*

1¼ yards of cream-with-multicolored-dots print for blocks and middle border

1⅛ yards of dark pink tone-on-tone print for blocks, sashing, inner border, and border corner squares

¾ yard of light yellow checked fabric for block backgrounds

⅝ yard of medium blue tone-on-tone print for blocks and flower center appliqués

⅜ yard of light blue tone-on-tone print for blocks, sashing squares, and flower appliqués

⅜ yard of medium yellow tone-on-tone print for flower appliqués

3⅝ yards of fabric for backing

60" x 77" piece of batting

1¾ yards of 16"-wide lightweight fusible web (optional)

34 red buttons, ½" diameter

*Yardage amount is for one-piece lengthwise-cut border strips. If you don't mind seams in your outer border, 1⅛ yards is sufficient to cut crosswise strips.

cutting

Cut all strips across the width of the fabric unless indicated otherwise.

From the cream-with-multicolored-dots print, cut:
3 strips, 6¾" x 42"; crosscut into 12 squares, 6¾" x 6¾". Cut each square into quarters diagonally to yield 48 triangles.

5 strips, 3¼" x 42"

From the medium blue tone-on-tone print, cut:
2 strips, 6¾" x 42"; crosscut into 6 squares, 6¾" x 6¾". Cut each square into quarters diagonally to yield 24 triangles.

From the dark pink tone-on-tone print, cut:
3 strips, 3⅝" x 42"; crosscut into 24 squares, 3⅝" x 3⅝". Cut each square in half diagonally to yield 48 triangles.

3 strips, 2⅛" x 42"

6 strips, 1⅞" x 42"; crosscut 4 of the strips into 7 strips, 1⅞" x 17"

4 squares, 5½" x 5½"

4 squares, 3¼" x 3¼"

From the light blue tone-on-tone print, cut:
2 strips, 3¼" x 42"; crosscut into 24 squares, 3¼" x 3¼"

2 squares, 1⅞" x 1⅞"

From the light yellow checked fabric, cut:
2 strips, 11½" x 42"; crosscut into 6 squares, 11½" x 11½"

From the dark red checked fabric, cut:
6 strips, 6" x 42"; crosscut into 34 squares, 6" x 6"

7 strips, 2" x 42"

From the *lengthwise grain* of the multicolored floral, cut:
2 strips, 5½" x 63"

2 strips, 5½" x 45" (or 6 strips, 5½" x 42", from the crosswise grain)

Pieced, appliquéd, and machine quilted by Nancy Mahoney

making the blocks

1. Lay out two multicolored-dots triangles and one medium blue triangle as shown. Sew the triangles together, offsetting the points ¼" as shown. Press the seam allowances as indicated. Make 24 units.

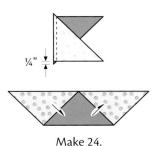

Make 24.

2. Sew dark pink triangles to the ends of each unit from step 1 as shown to complete the side units. Press the seam allowances toward the pink triangles.

Make 24.

3. Lay out four side units, four light blue 3¼" squares, and one light yellow square as shown. Sew the pieces together into rows and press the seam allowances as indicated. Sew the rows together and press the seam allowances as indicated. Make six blocks.

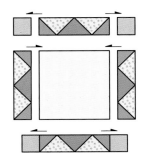

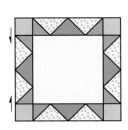

Make 6.

adding the appliqué

Use your preferred method or refer to "Appliqué" on page 5 for more information on starch appliqué and fusible-web machine appliqué. Refer to the diagram for appliqué placement.

1. Using the patterns on page 47 and your preferred method, make 48 red petals, 8 light blue petals, 28 medium yellow buds, and 10 medium blue circles.

2. Fold each block in half vertically and horizontally to establish centering lines. Working in numerical order, appliqué the shapes in place on each block. Set aside the light blue petals and the remaining yellow buds and blue circles for the border.

Appliqué placement

assembling the quilt top

1. Sew two blocks and one dark pink 17"-long sashing strip together as shown. Press the seam allowances toward the sashing strip. Make three block rows.

Make 3.

2. Sew two dark pink 17"-long sashing strips and one light blue 1⅞" square together as shown. Press the seam allowances toward the sashing strips. Make two sashing rows.

Make 2.

3. Refer to the quilt assembly diagram on page 46 to join the block rows and sashing rows. Press the seam allowances toward the sashing rows.

4. Join the dark pink 2⅛"-wide strips end to end to make a long strip. Refer to "Adding Borders" on page 10 to measure, cut, and sew inner-border

strips to the sides of the quilt top. Press the seam allowances toward the border strips. Using the dark pink 1⅞" x 42" strips, measure, cut, and sew inner-border strips to the top and bottom edges of the quilt top. Press the seam allowances toward the border strips.

5. To make the prairie points, fold each dark red 6" square in half diagonally, wrong sides together. Fold the square diagonally again, forming a smaller triangle. Make 34 prairie points.

Make 34.

6. Starting at one corner of the quilt, pin the cut edge of each prairie point to the cut edge of the quilt top, tucking the fold of one point into the opening of the next one. (They will overlap about ¼".) Make sure the folded edges of the triangles aim in the same direction as the first one and that the points are evenly spaced on each side. You should have 10 points on each side and seven points on the top and bottom of the quilt top. Using a walking foot and a scant ¼"-wide seam allowance, machine baste the prairie points to all four edges of the quilt top.

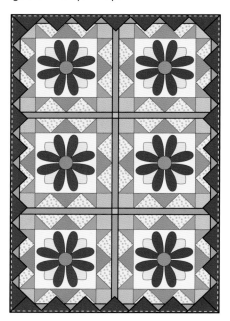

7. Measure the width of the quilt top and trim two of the multicolored-dots strips to that length. Join the three remaining multicolored-dots strips end to end to make a long strip. Measure the length of the quilt top and cut two strips to that length from the pieced strip. Sew the longer strips to the sides of the quilt top and press the seam allowances toward the inner border. Sew a dark pink 3¼" square to each end of the shorter strips. Press the seam allowances toward the pink squares. Sew the strips to the top and bottom edges of the quilt top. Press the seam allowances toward the inner border, with the prairie points pointing away from the quilt center.

8. Measure the length of the quilt top and trim the longer floral strips to that measurement for the side borders. Measure the width of the quilt top and trim the shorter floral strips to that measurement for the top and bottom borders. Sew the side borders to the quilt top. Add a dark pink 5½" square to each end of the shorter strips and sew them to the top and bottom edges of the quilt top for the outer border. Press the seam allowances toward the outer border.

Quilt assembly

9. Using the light blue petals, medium yellow buds, and medium blue circles you set aside earlier, appliqués the pieces in place as shown in the photo on page 44.

finishing

Refer to "Finishing Techniques" on page 11. Cut and piece the backing fabric, and then layer the quilt top with batting and backing. After basting the layers together, hand or machine quilt as desired; see the quilting suggestion at right. Trim the batting and backing so that the edges are even with the quilt top. Using the dark red 2"-wide strips, make and attach the binding. Center a button on each prairie point ¾" from the tip and stitch it in place through the top and batting layers only.

Quilting diagram

Patterns do not include seam allowances.

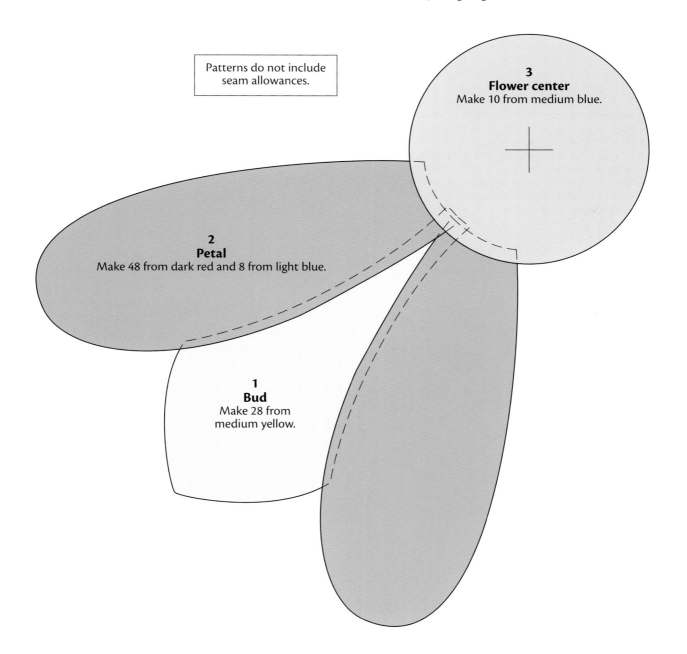

3
Flower center
Make 10 from medium blue.

2
Petal
Make 48 from dark red and 8 from light blue.

1
Bud
Make 28 from
medium yellow.

amaryllis

Big blocks and a simple border translate into an easy table topper or wall hanging. You'll have so much fun choosing your favorite flower colors that you'll want to make one for yourself and one as a gift for someone special.

Finished Quilt Size: 43½" x 43½"

Finished Block Size: 15" x 15"

materials

Yardages are based on 42"-wide fabrics. Fat quarters measure 18" x 21".

1⅜ yards of purple-and-gold floral for outer border*

1 fat quarter *each* of 4 assorted tan prints for block backgrounds

⅝ yard of green print for stem appliqués and binding

⅝ yard of medium purple print for flower appliqués

½ yard of dark purple print for inner border and flower appliqués

⅜ yard of yellow striped fabric for inner border and flower appliqués

3 yards of fabric for backing

50" x 50" piece of batting

3⅜ yards of 16"-wide lightweight fusible web (optional)

*Yardage amount is for one-piece lengthwise-cut border strips. If you don't mind seams in your outer border, ¾ yard is sufficient to cut crosswise strips.

cutting

Cut all strips across the width of the fabric unless indicated otherwise.

From *each* of the 4 assorted tan prints, cut:
1 square, 17" x 17"; cut into quarters diagonally to yield 4 triangles (16 total)

From the dark purple print, cut:
4 strips, 1¾" x 42"

From the yellow striped fabric, cut:
4 strips, 1¾" x 42"

From the *lengthwise grain* of the purple-and-gold floral, cut:
4 strips, 4½" x 45" (or 5 strips, 4½" x 42", from the crosswise grain)

From the green print, cut:
5 strips, 2" x 42"

making the blocks

Use your preferred method or refer to "Appliqué" on page 5 for more information on starch appliqué and fusible-web machine appliqué. Refer to the diagram on page 51 for appliqué placement.

1. Sew four different tan triangles together as shown to make an Hourglass block. Press the seam allowances open to reduce bulk. Make four blocks.

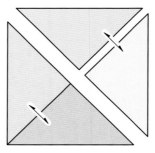 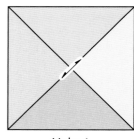

Make 4.

2. Using the patterns on page 52 and your preferred method, make 4 green stems, 16 dark purple flower tops, 16 yellow flower centers, and 16 medium purple lower flowers.

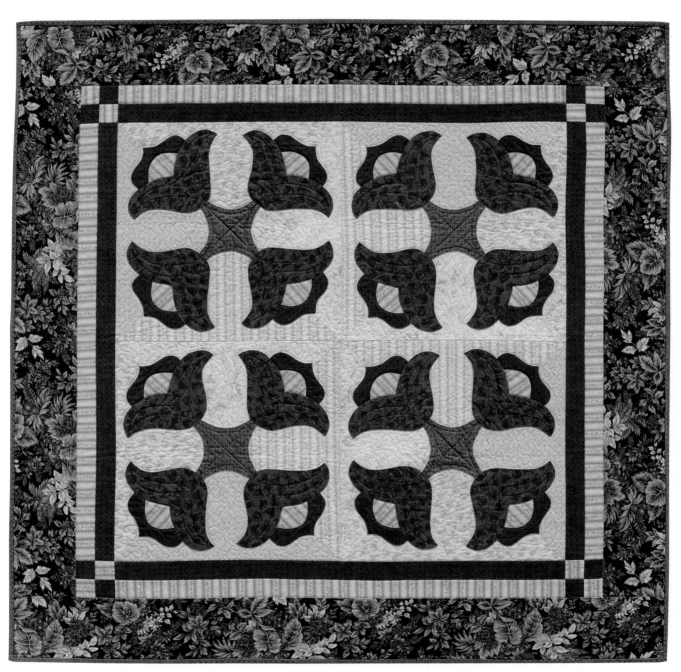

Pieced, appliquéd, and machine quilted by Nancy Mahoney

3. Using the seam lines as centering lines and working in numerical order, position the shapes on each block and appliqué them in place.

Appliqué placement

4. Trim each block to measure 15½" square, referring to "Squaring Up Blocks" on page 5.

making the four-patch units

1. Join a yellow strip to one long edge of a dark purple strip to make a strip set. Press the seam allowances toward the dark purple. Make four strip sets. From each strip set, crosscut two 1¾"-wide segments. Set the remainder of each strip set aside for the inner border.

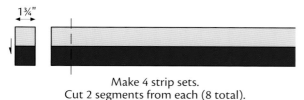

Make 4 strip sets.
Cut 2 segments from each (8 total).

2. Lay out two segments from step 1 as shown. Sew the segments together to make a four-patch unit. Press the seam allowances to one side. Make four units.

Make 4.

assembling the quilt top

1. Refer to the quilt assembly diagram to sew the blocks together in two rows of two blocks each. Press the seam allowances in opposite directions in each row. Sew the rows together. Press the seam allowances in one direction.

2. Refer to "Adding Borders" on page 10 to measure and cut four border strips from the remainder of the strip sets. Sew two strips to the sides of the quilt top. Sew a four-patch unit to each end of the

remaining two strips and sew them to the top and bottom edges of the quilt top for the inner border.

3. Using the purple-and-gold floral 4½"-wide strips, refer to "Adding Borders" to measure, cut, and sew the strips for the outer border, attaching them to the sides, and then to the top and bottom edges of the quilt top.

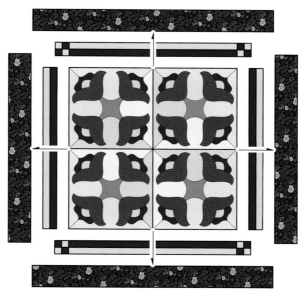

Quilt assembly

finishing

Refer to "Finishing Techniques" on page 11. Cut and piece the backing fabric, and then layer the quilt top with batting and backing. After basting the layers together, hand or machine quilt as desired; see the quilting suggestion below. Trim the batting and backing so that the edges are even with the quilt top. Using the green 2"-wide strips, make and attach the binding.

Quilting diagram

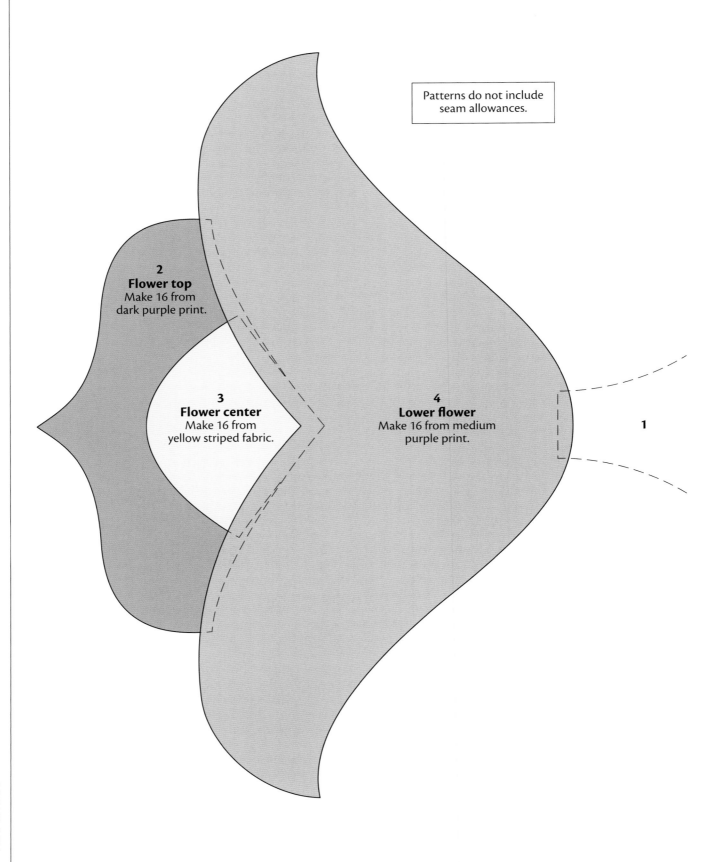

Patterns do not include seam allowances.

2
Flower top
Make 16 from dark purple print.

3
Flower center
Make 16 from yellow striped fabric.

4
Lower flower
Make 16 from medium purple print.

1

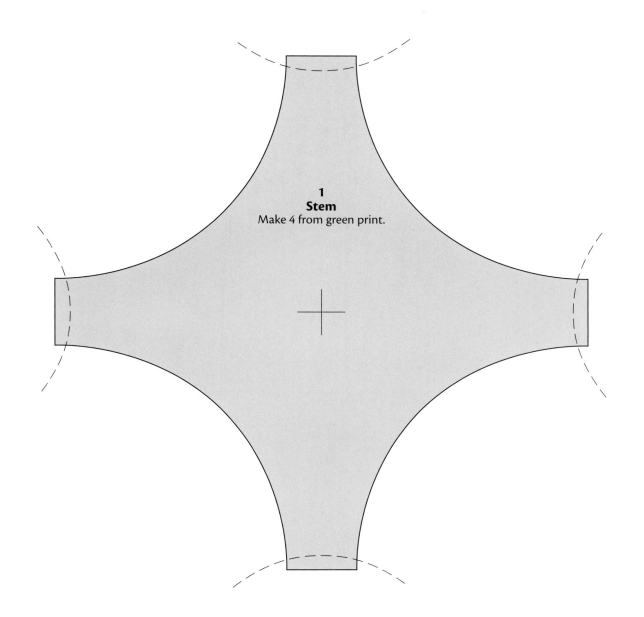

1
Stem
Make 4 from green print.

orange marmalade

This bold quilt will brighten any room. Wonderful Star blocks and easy appliqué combine to make a fresh, fun quilt—perfect for any teenage girl. Grab your bright fabrics and get ready to have a blast!

Finished Quilt Size: 65½" x 82½"
Finished Block Size: 12" x 12"

materials

Yardages are based on 42"-wide fabrics.

2⅓ yards of orange floral for blocks and outer border

1⅓ yards of white-on-white print for blocks

1 yard of light orange print for blocks and binding

⅔ yard of yellow mottled print for setting triangles

⅔ yard of green-on-white print 1 for blocks and setting triangles

⅔ yard of green-on-white print 2 for blocks and setting triangles

⅝ yard of light green print for blocks and inner border

½ yard of dark brown print for blocks

⅓ yard of dark pink print for blocks

⅓ yard of dark orange print for circle appliqués

⅓ yard of dark green print for leaf appliqués

5½ yards of fabric for backing

72" x 89" piece of batting

1⅛ yards of 16"-wide lightweight fusible web (optional)

cutting

Cut all strips across the width of the fabric unless indicated otherwise.

From the white-on-white print, cut:
9 strips, 4½" x 42"; crosscut into:
    48 squares, 4½" x 4½"
    48 rectangles, 2½" x 4½"

From the light green print, cut:
3 strips, 2½" x 42"; crosscut into 48 squares, 2½" x 2½"
7 strips, 1½" x 42"

From the dark pink print, cut:
3 strips, 2½" x 42"; crosscut into 48 squares, 2½" x 2½"

From the dark brown print, cut:
6 strips, 2½" x 42"; crosscut into 96 squares, 2½" x 2½"

From the light orange print, cut:
6 strips, 2½" x 42"; crosscut into 48 rectangles, 2½" x 4½"
8 strips, 2" x 42"

From the *lengthwise grain* of the orange floral, cut:
2 strips, 6½" x 75"
2 strips, 6½" x 70"
12 squares, 4½" x 4½"

From green-on-white print 1, cut:
3 strips, 6½" x 42"; crosscut into 18 squares, 6½" x 6½" (label as A)

From green-on-white print 2, cut:
3 strips, 6½" x 42"; crosscut into 16 squares, 6½" x 6½" (label as B)

From the yellow mottled print, cut:
2 strips, 9¾" x 42"; crosscut into:
    5 squares, 9¾" x 9¾"; cut each square into quarters diagonally to yield 20 side triangles
    2 squares, 9½" x 9½"; cut each square in half diagonally to yield 4 corner triangles

Pieced and appliquéd by Nancy Mahoney; machine quilted by Kelly Wise

making the star blocks

1. Draw a diagonal line from corner to corner on the wrong side of the light green and dark pink 2½" squares. Place a light green square on one corner of a white-on-white 4½" square, right sides together. Sew along the line and trim away the corner fabric, leaving a ¼" seam allowance. Press the seam allowances toward the white square. Make 48 units.

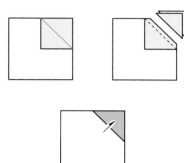

Make 48.

2. Repeat step 1, sewing a dark pink square to the diagonally opposite corner of each unit from step 1 to make 48 corner units. Press the seam allowances toward the resulting pink triangles.

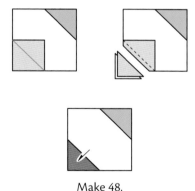

Make 48.

3. Draw a diagonal line from corner to corner on the wrong side of the dark brown 2½" squares. Place a marked square on one end of a white-on-white 2½" x 4½" rectangle, right sides together. Sew along the line and trim away the corner fabric, leaving a ¼" seam allowance. Press the seam allowances toward the resulting brown triangle.

In the same manner, add a marked square to the other end of the rectangle to make a flying-geese unit. Make 48 side units.

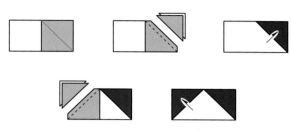

Make 48.

4. Sew a flying-geese unit to each light orange rectangle as shown to make a side unit. Press the seam allowances toward the orange rectangles. Make 48 side units.

Make 48.

5. Lay out four corner units, four side units, and one orange floral square in a nine-patch arrangement as shown. Sew the pieces together into rows and press the seam allowances as indicated. Sew the rows together; press. Make 12 blocks.

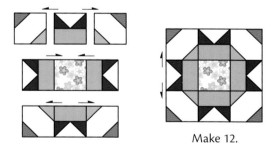

Make 12.

making the appliqué blocks

Use your preferred method or refer to "Appliqué" on page 5 for more information on starch appliqué and fusible-web machine appliqué. Refer to the diagram for appliqué placement.

1. Using the patterns on page 60 and your preferred method, make 40 dark orange circles, 34 dark green leaves, and 34 reversed dark green leaves.

2. Fold each green-on-white A square and B square in half vertically and horizontally to establish centering lines. Position the shapes on each

green-on-white square and appliqué them in place. Set aside six appliquéd A squares and four appliquéd B squares for the setting triangles.

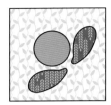

Appliqué placement

3. Lay out two A squares and two B squares in a four-patch arrangement as shown. Sew the squares together into rows, and then sew the rows together. Make six blocks. Press the seam allowances as indicated to reduce bulk.

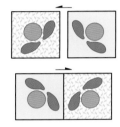 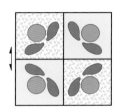

Make 6.

4. Appliqué a dark orange circle in the center of each block to complete the appliquéd blocks. Make six blocks.

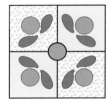

Make 6.

making the setting triangles

1. Sew yellow quarter-square triangles to adjacent sides of each of the remaining appliquéd A squares as shown. Press the seam allowances toward the yellow triangles. Make six setting triangles.

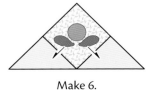

Make 6.

2. Sew yellow quarter-square triangles to adjacent sides of each of the remaining appliquéd B squares as shown. Press the seam allowances toward the yellow triangles. Make four setting triangles.

Make 4.

assembling the quilt top

1. Lay out the Star blocks, appliquéd blocks, appliquéd setting triangles, and yellow corner triangles in diagonal rows as shown. Position the appliquéd blocks and setting triangles so that the A squares are placed along the sides and the B squares are placed along the top and bottom of the quilt top. Sew the Star blocks, appliquéd blocks, and setting triangles together into rows, pressing the seam allowances toward the appliquéd blocks and triangles. Sew the rows together, matching seam intersections. Add the corner triangles and press. The corner triangles were cut a bit oversized for easier cutting and piecing. Trim and square up the quilt top, making sure to leave a ¼" seam allowance beyond the points of the Star blocks and appliquéd squares for seam allowances.

Quilt center layout

2. Join the light green 1½"-wide strips end to end to make a long strip. Refer to "Adding Borders" on page 10 and the quilt assembly diagram below to measure, cut, and sew the strips for the inner border, attaching them to the sides, and then to the top and bottom edges of the quilt center.

3. Using the orange floral 6½"-wide strips, measure and cut the longer strips and sew them to the sides of the quilt top. In the same manner, add the shorter strips to the top and bottom edges of the quilt top to complete the outer border.

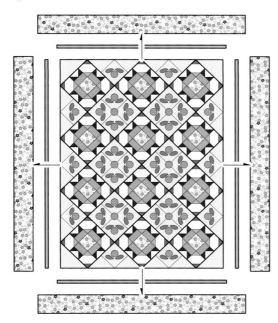

Quilt assembly

finishing

Refer to "Finishing Techniques" on page 11. Cut and piece the backing fabric, and then layer the quilt top with batting and backing. After basting the layers together, hand or machine quilt as desired; see the quilting suggestion below. Trim the batting and backing so that the edges are even with the quilt top. Using the light orange 2"-wide strips, make and attach the binding.

Quilting diagram

english garden

For a dramatically different look, use an elegant dark floral for the outer border. This romantic quilt will add beauty to any setting. Pieced and appliquéd by Nancy Mahoney; machine quilted by Dawn Kelly.

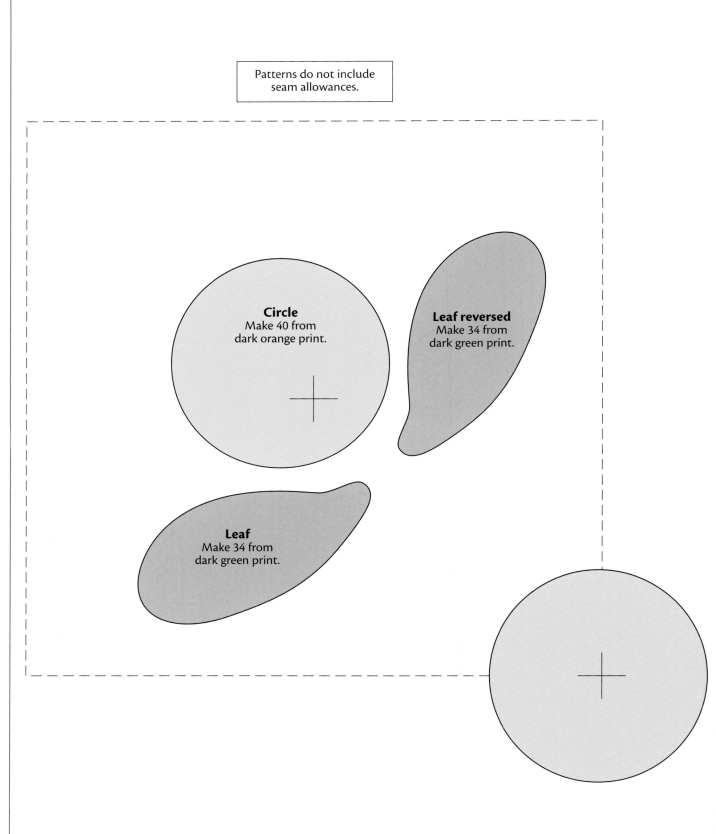

Patterns do not include
seam allowances.

Circle
Make 40 from
dark orange print.

Leaf reversed
Make 34 from
dark green print.

Leaf
Make 34 from
dark green print.

star flower baskets

Colorful baskets are brimming with bold star flowers in this delightful lap quilt. Easy pieced sashing and partial stars in the border provide the perfect showcase for the charming basket blocks.

Pieced, appliquéd, and machine quilted by Nancy Mahoney

Finished Quilt Size: 45½" x 65"

Finished Block Size: 9" x 11"

materials

Yardages are based on 42"-wide fabrics.

1⅝ yards of navy tone-on-tone print for sashing, sashing squares, and flower appliqués

1⅛ yards of tan print 1 for block backgrounds

1 yard of rust print for border, basket appliqués, and binding

1 yard of rust floral for border

⅜ yard of tan print 2 for sashing

¼ yard of green print for leaf appliqués

¼ yard of yellow print for flower-center appliqués

3⅛ yards of fabric for backing

52" x 71" piece of batting

3 yards of 16"-wide lightweight fusible web (optional)

cutting

Cut all strips across the width of the fabric.

From tan print 1, cut:
3 strips, 12" x 42"; crosscut into 12 rectangles, 10" x 12"

From the navy tone-on-tone print, cut:
2 strips, 3" x 42"; crosscut into 20 squares, 3" x 3"
20 strips, 1½" x 42"

From tan print 2, cut:
10 strips, 1" x 42"

From the rust floral, cut:
4 strips, 4½" x 42"

2 squares, 9¼" x 9¼"; cut each square into quarters diagonally to yield 8 triangles

4 squares, 4½" x 4½"

From the rust print, cut:
1 strip, 4⅞" x 42"; crosscut into 8 squares, 4⅞" x 4⅞". Cut each square in half diagonally to yield 16 triangles.

6 strips, 2" x 42"

appliquéing the blocks

Use your preferred method or refer to "Appliqué" on page 5 for more information on starch appliqué and fusible-web machine appliqué. Refer to the diagram for appliqué placement.

1. Using the patterns on page 65 and your preferred method, make 12 rust print basket handles, 12 rust print baskets, 36 green leaves, 36 navy star flowers, and 36 yellow flower centers.

2. Fold each tan print 1 rectangle in half vertically and horizontally to establish centering lines. Working in numerical order, position the shapes on each rectangle and appliqué them in place. Make 12 blocks.

Appliqué placement

3. Trim the blocks to measure 9½" x 11½", referring to "Squaring Up Blocks" on page 5.

assembling the quilt top

1. Join a navy strip to each long edge of a tan print 2 strip to make a strip set. Press the seam allowances toward the navy strips. Make 10 strip sets. Crosscut six of the strip sets into 16 segments, 11½" wide. Crosscut the remaining strip sets into 15 segments, 9½" wide.

11½"   9½"

Make 10 strip sets.
Cut 16 segments, 11½" wide,
and 15 segments, 9½" wide.

2. Sew three blocks and four 11½"-long sashing units together, alternating them as shown. Press the seam allowances toward the sashing strips. Make four block rows.

Make 4.

3. Sew three 9½"-long sashing units and four navy squares together, alternating them as shown. Press the seam allowances toward the sashing strips. Make five sashing rows.

Make 5.

4. Refer to the quilt assembly diagram to join the block rows and sashing rows. Press the seam allowances toward the sashing rows. The quilt top should measure 37½" x 57".

adding the border

1. Sew rust print triangles to the short sides of each rust floral triangle as shown to make flying-geese units. Press the seam allowances away from the floral triangles. Make eight units, measuring 4½" x 8½".

Make 8.

2. Sew the rust floral strips together in pairs to make two long strips. Cut each strip into one 41"-long strip and one 21½"-long strip.

3. Sew a flying-geese unit from step 1 to each end of the 41"-long strips. Press the seam allowances toward the rust floral and sew the strips to the sides of the quilt top as shown. Press the seam allowances toward the navy sashing strips.

4. Sew a flying-geese unit from step 1 to each end of the 21½"-long strips. Press the seam allowances toward the rust floral. Then sew a rust floral square to each end of the strips and press the seam

allowances toward the squares. Sew the strips to the top and bottom of the quilt top as shown for the outer border.

Quilt assembly

finishing

Refer to "Finishing Techniques" on page 11. Cut and piece the backing fabric, and then layer the quilt top with batting and backing. After basting the layers together, hand or machine quilt as desired; see the quilting suggestion below. Trim the batting and backing so that the edges are even with the quilt top. Using the rust print 2"-wide strips, make and attach the binding.

Quilting diagram

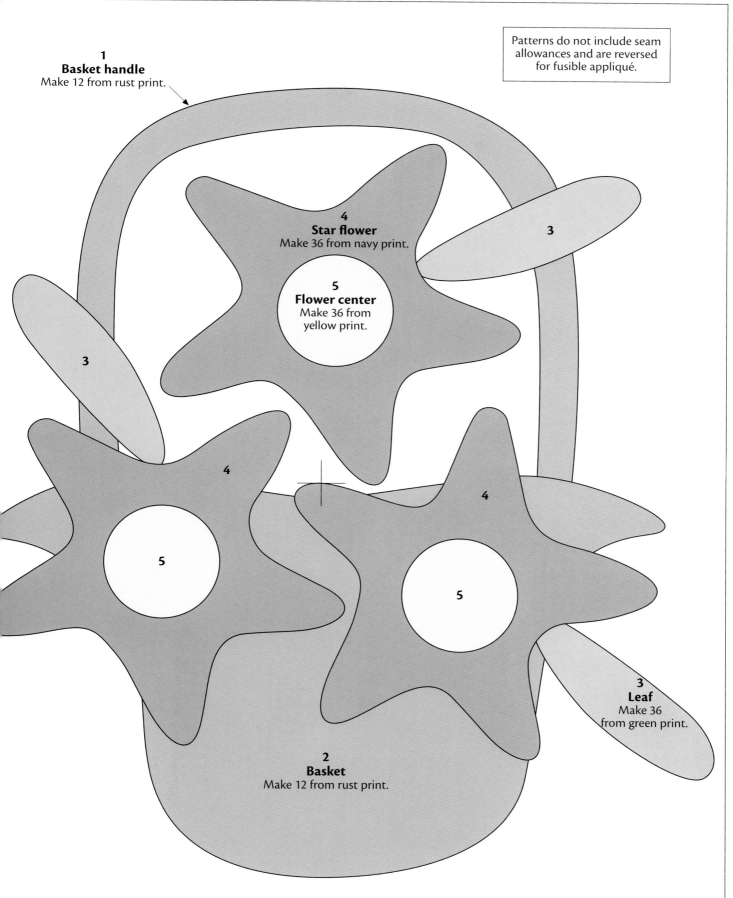

1
Basket handle
Make 12 from rust print.

Patterns do not include seam allowances and are reversed for fusible appliqué.

4
Star flower
Make 36 from navy print.

3

5
Flower center
Make 36 from yellow print.

3

4

5

4

5

3
Leaf
Make 36
from green print.

2
Basket
Make 12 from rust print.

daisy vines

A field of daisies always makes me smile, as do the slightly whimsical daisies in this happy, sunny quilt! A variety of beige prints in the background add a visually fascinating dimension, while simple appliqué guarantees that the quilt is suitable for all skill levels.

Finished Quilt Size: 43½" x 53½"

materials

Yardages are based on 42"-wide fabrics. Fat quarters measure 18" x 21" and fat eighths measure 9" x 21".

1¾ yards of navy checked fabric for flower appliqués, outer border, and binding

⅞ yard of green print for vine appliqués, leaf appliqués, and inner border corner squares

1 fat quarter *each* of 3 assorted beige prints for appliqué background

⅓ yard of medium blue mottled print for sashing, inner border, and border flower appliqués

1 fat quarter of light blue floral for sashing and inner border

1 fat quarter of light blue checked fabric for sashing and inner border

1 fat eighth of yellow mottled print for flower appliqués

3 yards of fabric for backing

50" x 60" piece of batting

1⅛ yards of 16"-wide lightweight fusible web (optional)

⅜" bias bar for vines

cutting

Cut all strips across the width of the fabric unless indicated otherwise.

From *each* of the 3 assorted beige fat quarters, cut:
16 rectangles, 4" x 5" (48 total)

From the light blue floral, cut:
2 rectangles, 3" x 9½"
2 rectangles, 3" x 7"
4 rectangles, 3" x 6½"

From the light blue checked fabric, cut:
3 rectangles, 3" x 9½"
3 rectangles, 3" x 7"
4 rectangles, 3" x 6½"

From the medium blue mottled print, cut:
3 rectangles, 3" x 9½"
3 rectangles, 3" x 7"
4 rectangles, 3" x 6½"

From the green print, cut:
Enough 1¼"-wide bias strips to total 230" in length when joined end to end
4 squares, 3" x 3"

From the navy checked fabric, cut:
6 strips, 2" x 42"

From the *lengthwise grain* of the remaining navy checked fabric, cut:
4 strips, 6½" x 45"

Pieced, appliquéd, and machine quilted by Nancy Mahoney

making the appliquéd strips

Use your preferred method or refer to "Appliqué" on page 5 for more information on starch appliqué and fusible-web machine appliqué. Refer to the diagram for appliqué placement.

1. Randomly sew together four beige rectangles to make a four-patch unit as shown. Press the seam allowances to one side (or press them open to reduce bulk). Make 12 units.

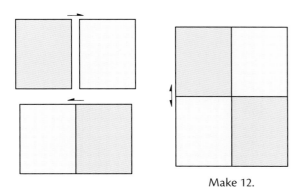

Make 12.

2. Randomly sew four units from step 1 together to make a vertical row. Press the seam allowances open. Make three rows.

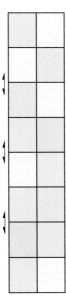

Make 3.

3. Using the patterns on page 71 and your preferred method, make 60 navy petals, 20 medium blue petals, 54 green leaves, and 16 yellow flower centers. Set aside the medium blue petals, 36 leaves, and 4 flower centers for the border appliqués.

4. Join the green 1¼"-wide bias strips end to end to make a 230"-long strip. Fold the strip in half, wrong sides together, and stitch a *scant* ¼" from the raw edges. Trim the seam allowance to ⅛". Slide the bias bar inside the fabric tube. Twist the fabric until the seam is centered along one flat side of the bias bar. Press the tube flat, with the seam allowances pressed to one side. Gently work the bias bar through the tube, pressing as you go. When the entire tube has been pressed, remove the bias bar and gently press the tube again.

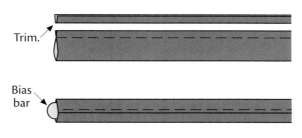

Trim.

Bias bar

5. Cut the fabric tube into two 43"-long vines, two 34"-long vines, and nine 8"-long vines.

6. Starting with the 8"-long vines, and working in numerical order, position the shapes along the center of each vertical row and appliqué them in place. Make three vertical rows.

8"

Appliqué placement

assembling the quilt top

1. Using the light blue floral, light blue checked, and medium blue mottled 3" x 6½" rectangles, lay out two rectangles of each print as shown. Join the rectangles end to end to make a sashing strip. Press the seam allowances to one side (or press them open to reduce bulk). Make two.

Make 2.

2. Refer to the quilt assembly diagram to sew the appliquéd block rows and sashing strips together, alternating them as shown. Press the seam allowances toward the sashing strips.

adding the borders

1. Using the light blue floral, light blue checked, and medium blue mottled 3" x 9½" rectangles, sew together four rectangles to make a side border strip. Refer to the photo on page 68 as needed for placement guidance. Press the seam allowances open. Make two strips.

2. Using the light blue floral, light blue checked, and medium blue mottled 3" x 7" rectangles, sew together four rectangles to make a top border strip. Again, refer to the photo as needed for placement guidance. Press the seam allowances open. Repeat to make a bottom border strip. Sew green squares to the ends of these two short border strips. Sew the border strips to the sides, and then to the top and bottom edges of the quilt top for the inner border. Press the seam allowances toward the border.

3. Refer to "Adding Borders" on page 10 to measure, cut, and sew the navy checked 6½"-wide strips to the sides, and then to the top and bottom edges of the quilt top for the outer border.

Quilt assembly

4. Using the prepared appliqué pieces and vines, and working in numerical order, position the shapes on the outer border and appliqué them in place.

finishing

Refer to "Finishing Techniques" on page 11. Cut and piece the backing fabric, and then layer the quilt top with batting and backing. After basting the layers together, hand or machine quilt as desired; see the quilting suggestion at right. Trim the batting and backing so that the edges are even with the quilt top. Using the navy checked 2"-wide strips, make and attach the binding.

Quilting diagram

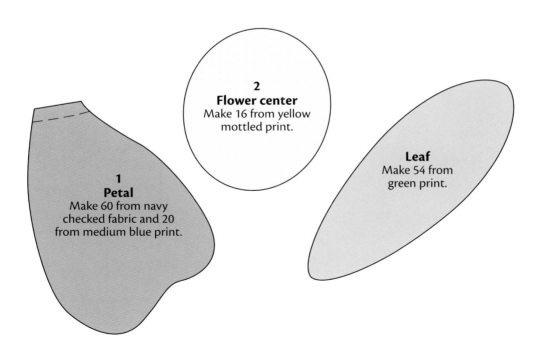

Patterns do not include seam allowances and are reversed for fusible appliqué.

2
Flower center
Make 16 from yellow mottled print.

Leaf
Make 54 from green print.

1
Petal
Make 60 from navy checked fabric and 20 from medium blue print.

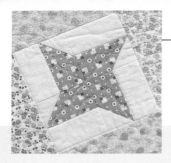

pinwheel flowers

Easy patchwork techniques make short work of these tricky-looking blocks. I chose 1930s-era reproduction fabrics, but imagine this design in a rich assortment of batiks, earth-toned fabrics, or holiday colors. The possibilities are endless!

Finished Quilt Size: 46½" x 54½"
Finished Block Size: 8" x 8"

materials

Yardages are based on 42"-wide fabrics. Fat eighths measure 9" x 21".

1½ yards of yellow print for middle border*

1 fat eighth *each* of 9 assorted medium or dark prints for blocks and folded hexagon flowers

1 fat eighth *each* of 9 assorted light background prints for blocks

1 yard of cream solid for blocks

⅞ yard of green print for blocks, outer border, and binding

⅓ yard of light floral for blocks and inner border

3¼ yards of fabric for backing

53" x 61" piece of batting

5 yards of green medium-width rickrack for vine

24 yellow buttons, about ½" diameter

Ladybug, bee, or other novelty buttons (optional)

Fabric glue (optional)

Yardage amount is for one-piece lengthwise-cut borders. If you don't mind seams in your outer border, ⅞ yard is sufficient to cut crosswise strips.

cutting

Cut all strips across the width of the fabric, unless indicated otherwise.

From the cream solid, cut:
14 strips, 2" x 42"; crosscut into:
    20 strips, 2" x 21"
    80 squares, 2" x 2"

From *each* of the 9 assorted medium or dark fat eighths, cut:
2 strips, 2" x 21" (18 total)

From the remainder of the assorted medium or dark fat eighths, cut a total of:
24 circles (pattern on page 77)

From the green print, cut:
5 strips, 2¼" x 42"

7 strips, 2" x 42"; crosscut *1 strip* into 2 strips, 2" x 21". Set aside the remainder of the strips for the binding.

From *each* of the assorted light background fat eighths, cut:
2 strips, 3½" x 21"; crosscut into 4 rectangles, 3½" x 8" (36 total)

From the light floral, cut:
1 strip, 3½" x 42"; crosscut into 4 rectangles, 3½" x 8"
4 strips, 1¼" x 42"

From the *lengthwise grain* of the yellow print, cut:
4 strips, 5" x 46" (or 5 strips, 5" x 42", from the crosswise grain)

Pieced and machine quilted by Nancy Mahoney

making the blocks

1. Using the 2"-wide strips, sew a medium or dark print strip and a cream strip together along their long edges to make a strip set. Press the seam allowances toward the print strip. Make 20 strip sets. Crosscut each strip set into four 3½"-wide segments (80 total). Keep the four matching segments from each strip set together.

3½"

Make 20 strip sets.
Cut 4 segments from each strip set (80 total).

2. Draw a diagonal line on the wrong side of each cream square. Place a cream square on one print corner of a segment from step 1 as shown. Sew along the line and trim away the corner fabric, leaving a ¼" seam allowance. Press the seam allowances toward the resulting cream triangle. Make 80 units. Keep the matching units together.

Make 4 matching
units (80 total).

3. Lay out four matching units in a four-patch arrangement as shown. Sew the units together into rows, and then sew the rows together. Press the seam allowances as indicated to reduce bulk. Make 20 star units.

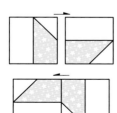 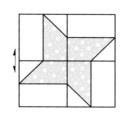

Make 20.

4. With the *right side facing up*, cut each light 3½" x 8" rectangle diagonally as shown to make 80 long triangles. Make sure you cut each rectangle exactly as shown, or your blocks will tilt in the wrong direction.

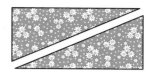

Cut 80 long triangles.

5. Randomly select and sew long triangles to opposite sides of each star unit from step 3, offsetting the triangles ¼" as shown. Press the seam allowances toward the triangles. Sew long triangles to the remaining two sides of the block and press. Make 20 blocks. Trim each block to 8½" x 8½", making sure to leave ¼" beyond the points on all sides for seam allowances.

¼"

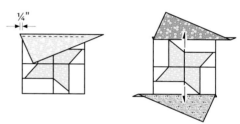

Trim.

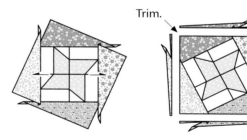

Make 20.

assembling the quilt top

1. Lay out the block in five rows of four blocks each. When you're pleased with the arrangement, sew the blocks together into rows and press the seam allowances in opposite directions from row to row. Sew the rows together and press the seam allowances in one direction.

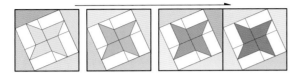

2. Refer to "Adding Borders" on page 10 and the quilt assembly diagram to measure, cut, and sew the light floral 1¼"-wide strips for the inner border, attaching them to the sides, and then to the top and bottom edges of the quilt top. Press the seam allowances toward the border strips.

3. Repeat step 2 to measure, cut, and sew the yellow 5"-wide strips for the middle border. Press the seam allowances toward the just-added border strips.

4. Join the green 2¼"-wide strips together end to end to make a long strip. Measure, cut, and sew the strips for the outer border, attaching them to the sides, and then to the top and bottom edges of the quilt top. Press the seam allowances toward the just-added border strips.

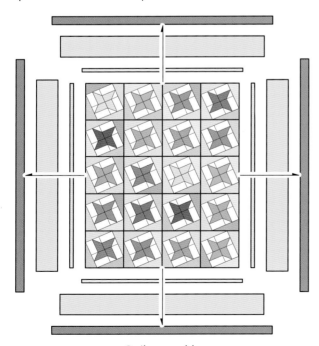

Quilt assembly

5. For the rickrack vine, arrange the green rickrack on the middle border in a meandering line as shown in the photo on page 74. Pin or glue in place, and then use matching thread to topstitch through the center of the rickrack vine.

finishing

Refer to "Finishing Techniques" on page 11. Cut and piece the backing fabric, and then layer the quilt top with batting and backing. After basting the layers together, hand or machine quilt as desired; see the quilting suggestion below. Trim the batting and backing so that the edges are even with the quilt top. Using the green 2"-wide strips, make and attach the binding.

Quilting diagram

adding the flowers

1. Fold a medium or dark circle into quarters and lightly press to make centering lines. With the *wrong side* facing up, fold one edge of the circle to the center line as shown and press the fold.

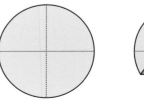

Press.   Fold and press.

2. Fold one of the just-created points to the center; press the fold. Continue folding points to the center and pressing to complete a hexagon flower. Make 24 flowers.

3. After the quilting is completed, arrange the flowers along the rickrack vine as shown in the photo on page 74. Sew a yellow button in the center of each flower, and then sew the flower to the quilt top along the flower's outer edges. Add novelty buttons to the yellow border as desired.

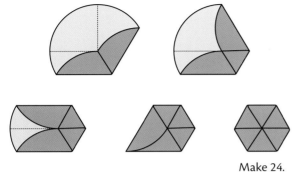

Make 24.

Pattern does not include seam allowance.

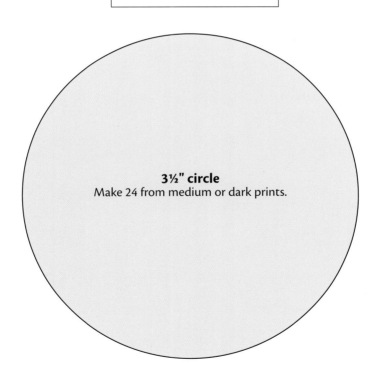

3½" circle
Make 24 from medium or dark prints.

acknowledgments

A very special thanks to:

Tom Reichert, for giving me time to do what I love, even when it meant that there was less time for other things. Your never-ending support and encouragement make all things possible!

The wonderful people at Martingale & Company; your team of dedicated women and men are always a joy to work with! Thank you for producing books I can be proud of.

Nannette Moore and Kelly Wise, machine quilters extraordinaire.

Kathy, Kelly, Jan, Melanie, and everyone at the Sew and Quilt Shop in Bunnell, Florida—a great bunch of gals!

The Memory Makers Quilt Guild—a delightful group of women, whose enthusiasm always inspires me.

The following companies, who generously provided so many great products: P&B Textiles, whose lovely fabrics created so many of the quilts; Sulky threads and adhesives; Fairfield for its wonderful Soft Touch batting; Prym Dritz for its rulers and other exceptional products; and the Warm Company for its outstanding fusible-web products.

about the author

An author, teacher, fabric designer, and award-winning quiltmaker, Nancy Mahoney has enjoyed making quilts for more than 20 years. An impressive range of her beautiful quilts has been featured in more than 90 national and international quilt magazines.

This is Nancy's eleventh book with Martingale & Company. Her previous best sellers include *Treasures from the '30s* (2010), *Ribbon Star Quilts* (2008), *Appliqué Quilt Revival* (2008), and *Quilt Revival* (2006).

When she's not designing and making quilts, Nancy enjoys traveling to guilds and events around the country, sharing her quilts, teaching her piecing and machine-appliqué techniques, and visiting gardens.

Nancy makes her home in Florida with her life partner of more than 30 years, Tom, and their umbrella cockatoo, Prince.

there's more online!

Find free patterns, workshop and lecture listings, beautiful quilts, and more at www.nancymahoney.com.

Discover more terrific quilting, knitting, crochet, and crafts books at www.martingale-pub.com.

you might also enjoy these other fine titles from
Martingale & Company

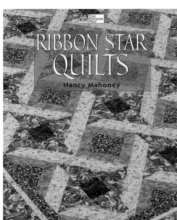

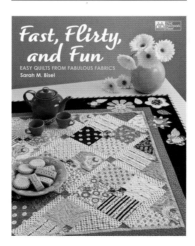

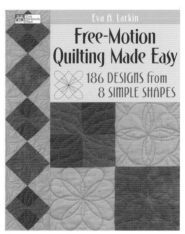

Our books are available at bookstores and your favorite craft, fabric, and yarn retailers.
Visit us at www.martingale-pub.com or contact us at:

1-800-426-3126
International: 1-425-483-3313
Fax: 1-425-486-7596
Email: info@martingale-pub.com

Martingale®
& COMPANY

America's Best-Loved Craft & Hobby Books®
America's Best-Loved Knitting Books®